NEVER SAY DIE:
A Survival Manual

PALADIN
press

Post Office Box 1307
Boulder, Colorado 80306

TABLE OF CONTENTS

SURVIVAL
PSYCHOLOGY

CHAPTER 1

PSYCHOLOGICAL ASPECTS OF SURVIVAL

INTRODUCTION

In recent years many advances have been made in the development of clothing, equipment, and rations for survival and of techniques for their use. However, regardless of how good equipment is or how good the techniques for its use are, the man faced with a survival situation still has himself to deal with. Man's psychological reactions to the stresses of survival often make him unable to utilize his available resources.

The information available in this field is far from complete but enough has been done to give an understanding of some of the major psychological factors involved in survival. While much of this information could be labelled common sense, it should be remembered that common sense is based on past experiences which have led to successful adjustments to various situations and that inability to use common sense under stress had led to the deaths of many very able, apparently sensible persons.

One of the most important psychological requirements for survival is the ability to accept immediately the reality of a new emergency and react appropriately to it.

Studies have demonstrated that survival information contributes to a feeling of confidence in one's ability to survive. Since self-confidence is important in handling fear and panic, survival information should serve to minimize fear and prevent panic.

Survival training should have in it some elements of realism like "battle inoculation" but safeguards must be taken against the production of casualties. Men must feel that they have come through real danger but have escaped unharmed.

Fear

Fear is a very normal reaction for any man faced with an emergency which threatens any of his important needs. Fear influences man's behaviour and thus his chances for survival; fear may ruin his chances or

11

may actually improve them. There is no advantage in avoiding fear by denying the existence of danger. There is always something that can be done to improve the situation. Acceptance of fear as a natural reaction to a threatening situation will lead to purposive rather than random behaviour and in this way will greatly increase chances for survival.

How a person will react to fear depends more on himself than on the situation. It isn't always the physically strong or happy-go-lucky person who most effectively handles fear; timid or anxious persons may respond more coolly and effectively under stress with a resulting better chance for survival. Fear must be recognized, lived with, and if possible, utilized to advantage.

Factors increasing fear are mainly helplessness and hopelessness. Some of the factors most frequently reported to decrease or help control fear are:

(a) having confidence in your equipment;

(b) having confidence in the technical ability of your immediate superior; and

(c) concentrating on the job to be done.

Seven Enemies of Survival

Pain, cold, thirst, hunger, fatigue, boredom, and loneliness—everyone has experienced these but few have known them to the extent that they have threatened survival. In the survival situation, the feelings of pain, cold, etc., are no different from those experienced elsewhere. They are only more severe and more dangerous. With these feelings, as with fear, the more you know about them and their effects on you, the better you will be able to control them, rather than letting them control you.

(a) Pain. Pain is Nature's way of making you pay attention to something that is wrong with you. But Nature also has ways of holding off pain if you are too busy doing something else to pay attention to the injury right then. Pain may go unnoticed if your mind is occupied with plans for survival. On the other hand, once given in to, pain will weaken the drive to survive. Pain can get the best of you if you let it, even if it isn't serious or prolonged. A special effort must be made to keep hopes up and to keep working.

(b) Cold. Cold is a much greater threat to survival than it sounds. It not only lowers your ability to think, but also tends to lower your will to do anything but get warm again. Cold is an insidious enemy; at the same time that it numbs the mind and the body, it numbs the will. Because it is hard to move and you want to sleep, you can forget your goal . . . . to survive.

(c) Thirst. Thirst is another enemy of survival. Even when thirst is not extreme, it can dull your mind. As with pain and cold, thirst can be almost forgotten if the will to survive is strong enough. It is also important to remember not to deprive oneself unnecessarily of water. Serious dehydration may occur in a survival situation even when there is plenty of water available.

(d) Hunger. Hunger is dangerous because of the effects it can have on the mind, primarily in lessening the person's ability for rational thought. Both thirst and hunger increase a person's susceptibility to the weakening effects of cold, pain, and fear.

(e) Fatigue. Even a very moderate amount of fatigue can materially reduce mental ability. Fatigue can make you careless—it becomes increasingly easy to adopt the feeling of just not caring. This is one of the biggest dangers in survival. The confused notion that fatigue and energy expenditure are directly related may be responsible for many deaths in survival situations. Certainly, there is a real danger of over-exertion, but fatigue may actually be due to hopelessness, lack of a goal, dissatisfaction, frustration, or boredom. Fatigue may represent an escape from a situation which has become too difficult. If you recognize the dangers of a situation, you can often summon the strength to go on.

(f) Boredom and Loneliness. Boredom and loneliness are two of the toughest enemies of survival. They are bad mainly because they are unexpected. When nothing happens, when something is expected and doesn't come off, when you must stay still, quiet, and alone, these feelings creep up on you.

Attitudes for Survival

While some attitudes are actually essential to survival there are others which greatly endanger chances of survival. For example, the mental attitude that "it can't happen to me" can blind you to the reality of the situation and make appropriate reaction in the face of emergency impossible.

Much of the available evidence demonstrates the importance of having a "preparatory attitude" for whatever emergency may occur. This leads to preparation and rehearsal for all emergency possibilities. Survival instructions, given through posters, movies, lectures, etc, have been found to produce preparatory attitudes for survival which later serve as guides to action. Either general or specific information may serve this purpose. Often knowledge of the experience of others has also served as preparation for action. A great number of incidents have been recorded which indicate that previous rehearsal, both mental and actual, of emergency procedures may operate as preparation resulting in automatic action.

The most frequently encountered attitude endangering survival is the "it can't happen to me" attitude. This is the opposite of the preparatory attitude.

Failure to have an attitude for survival may also result in panic, even in persons who appear to be extremely calm under normal conditions.

Knowledge and rehearsal of survival and emergency procedure not only bring about a feeling of confidence and preparation for survival, but they can operate even when the survivor is in a state of semi-consciousness during an emergency.

Group Behaviour in Survival

Group Organization. A crew's chances of surviving depend largely on its ability to organize activity. An emergency does not weld a crew together; rather, the more difficult and disordered the situation, the greater are the disorganized crew's problems. This is particularly true in the face of common danger, when fear can result in panic rather than concentration.

Group Morale. High group morale exists when all crew members feel themselves part of the crew rather than individuals, and are proud to be members of that crew. High group morale has many advantages.

(a) The individual feels strengthened and protected since he realizes that his survival depends on others whom he trusts.

(b) The group can meet failure with greater persistency.

(c) The group can formulate goals to help each other face the future.

High morale must come from internal cohesiveness and not merely through external pressures. Under certain conditions, moods and attitudes become wildly contagious. Panic often may be prevented by conscious, well-planned organization and leadership on the basis of delegated or shared responsibility, combined with faith in the group and realization of the need for co-operation.

Important Factors in Successful Group Survival

(a) Organization of manpower. Organized action, when crew members know what to do and when to do it, both under ordinary circumstances and in emergencies, is one good way of combating panic. An important technique for achieving organized action in survival is to keep the crew well briefed.

(b) Selective Use of Personnel. In well-organized groups, the person often does the job that most closely fits his personal qualifications.

(c) Acceptance of Suggestions and Criticisms. Although some one person, such as the aircraft commander, must accept responsibility for final decisions, he still can make good use of others' suggestions and criticisms.

(d) Consideration of Available Time. Hundreds of survival stories indicate that there is rarely unlimited time in which to make decisions. On-the-spot decisions which must be acted upon immediately usually determine survival success.

14

(e) Checking Equipment. In many more cases than will ever be known, failure to check equipment resulted in failure to survive.

(f) Surveying the Situation. The necessity for surveying the situation is widely recognized in problem solving. Frequently the things most feared are those involving the unknown. Surveying the situation serves to remove those unknowns and to set in readiness powers of adjustment.

(g) Survival Knowledge and Skills. Research has shown that confidence in one's ability to survive is increased by acquiring survival knowledge and skills.

(h) Reaction Speed. In survival emergencies, previously established reaction patterns are important in enabling the group to react quickly. It is claimed that one main purpose of survival training is to afford an opportunity for knowing and understanding the responses persons and groups need to acquire. Well established patterns of response may operate even when there is shock and panic.

Personality Requirements of Survival

Survival may depend more upon personality than upon the danger, weather, terrain, or nature of the emergency. Whether fear will lead to panic or act as a spur to greater sharpness, whether fatigue will overcome the person or leave him able to take the necessary action to survive, even whether or not he will have frost-bitten feet, all are, to a large extent, dependent more on the person than on the situation. Qualities in a man important to survival are as follows.

(a) He can make up his mind.

(b) He can improvise.

(c) He can live with himself. Some people can't stand being alone, have to be entertained, etc. Others can take care of themselves, make a good thing out of a bad one, keep their own and others' spirits up.

(d) He can adapt to the situation. Some people can't change themselves, no matter how much their stubbornness costs.

(e) He can keep cool, calm, and collected.

(f) He hopes for the best, but prepares for the worst.

(g) He has patience. Some people must do everything right now. Others are able to wait until they have a surer chance.

(h) He can take it. Few people know how much they can really take, but expecting things to be tough or unpleasant helps any of us to be prepared to meet the worst that can happen.

(j) He can figure out the other man. Some men step on everybody's toes, while others manage to keep practically everybody happy. The principal reason that this second group of men is so successful is that they are always aware of the feelings and moods of other people. This ability to understand other people and to predict what they are going to do is important to survival.

(k) He knows where his special fears and worries come from. All of us had accidents, scares, and worries when we were children that still bother us. Under dangerous survival conditions, these may cause trouble, but if a man knows where they came from, he can do something to control them.

SURVIVAL
GEOGRAPHY

Chapter 2

SURVIVAL GEOGRAPHY

INTRODUCTION

Geography in the survival sense must be somewhat restricted in scope. This is because a survivor will be interested only in the aspects of geography that directly pertain to him. The survival concept of geography may differ also from that of the botanist or the cartographer. For example, the Arctic is commonly considered to include everything north of the Arctic circle, i.e., everything above latitude 66°32′ whereas the survival definition of the Arctic includes everything north of the tree-line.

The aim of survival geography is to teach the survival student what to expect from the land, wherever he may be. A survivor who knows what to expect will find that his problems are greatly reduced, for he should then know what to do. Once a survivor settles down to improving his situation, he will also improve his morale and strengthen his will to live.

Topography affects temperature, humidity, and water sheds which in turn influence the plant growth. The plant growth largely determines the animal life which can exist in any geographic region. The carnivorous predators, in their turn, depend on the seed and plant eaters and they consequently live a somewhat precarious existence which may be terminated by a change in any one of a number of factors.

The following map shows a simplified division of Canada's forested and non-forested regions. The break-down is made into eight parts, four of which are particularly important from a survival point of view. The remaining four parts are covered in order to fill in the background with additional information that may be useful. The emphasis is on northern survival because of the strategic and economic development of and the ever increasing amount of flying being done over Canada's northland.

It may be readily seen that the Boreal Region is the largest forest region in Canada. This region occupies a major part of the Canadian Shield, a massive formation of eroded palaeozoic rock, sparsely covered with a poor topsoil, which is unsuitable for agriculture but highly satisfactory for the growth of certain trees. A large portion of Canada's forest

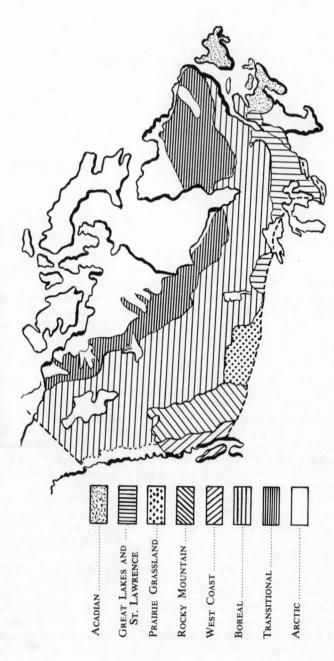

FOREST CLASSIFICATION OF CANADA

ACADIAN ....

GREAT LAKES AND
ST. LAWRENCE ......

PRAIRIE GRASSLAND ......

ROCKY MOUNTAIN ......

WEST COAST ......

BOREAL ......

TRANSITIONAL ......

ARCTIC ......

wealth occupies the Canadian Shield and this great forest region shows remarkably little variation from one coast to the other. This is because the factors which influence forest growth and development, such as soil, temperature, humidity, and sunlight, remain relatively constant across this entire region. When one factor, e.g., temperature, does vary, it will be found that another factor, e.g., humidity, tends to compensate and the net result is the same or a similar type of growth.

Local variations will be found, however, and changes will occur, in the plant life within regions. The changes may be caused by such things as fire, disease, cutting, and even normal growth. In any event, the plant eating insects, birds, and animals will be affected by such variations, and the predator population will also vary according to the increase or decrease in the number of the various types of plant eaters.

Bearing in mind, then, that local variations are inevitable, the following generalized information which necessarily omits much detail, is offered as a guide to survival geography.

Acadian (Maritimes and Newfoundland)

Topography and soil—includes part of the Appalachians; picturesque, rolling hills; wide river valleys.

Watersheds—scattered small lakes well drained by extensive networks of moderately flowing streams and rivers.

Climate and humidity—averages 55 inches of rain a year; temperatures moderate; few extremes except in inland areas.

Plant life—spruce, balsam, yellow birch, maple, and pine; very similar to the Boreal Region.

Wild life—trout, salmon, shad, ale-wife, eel, sucker, and chub; red squirrel, varying hare, porcupine, muskrat, beaver, weasel, mink, otter, fox, lynx, panther, black bear, deer, and moose; pheasant, partridge, grouse, duck, hawk, owl, eagle, gull, crow, and raven.

Great Lakes and St. Lawrence

Topography and soil—mostly peneplain; Canada's biggest fruit and vegetable growing district.

Watersheds—short, moderately flowing rivers drain into the Great Lakes and St. Lawrence.

Climate and humidity—quite humid, mostly over 50 inches of rain a year; temperatures not very extreme.

Plant life—white and red pine, spruce, yellow birch, and maple.

Wild life—deer, grey and black squirrel, cotton-tail rabbit, jack rabbit, porcupine, fox, racoon, and musk-rat; hawk, owl, and pheasant; turtle, pike, smelt, perch, walleye, bass, catfish, and carp.

Prairie Grassland

Topography and soil—the Great Plains are mostly very flat and have, except for broken up bad lands, in the south-west corner, extremely deep soil.

Watersheds—innumerable scattered sloughs and small lakes; slow flowing rivers in deep coulees; often wide valleys.

Climate and humidity—dry climate, 10 inches of rain in the west to 20 inches in the east; the temperature varies to extremes.

Plant life—grasses, sedges, bullrushes, and bushes.

Wild life—porcupine, gopher, prairie dog, rabbit, badger, coyote, deer, antelope, and elk; prairie chicken, hawk, owl, duck, and geese; pike, jackfish, trout, and white-fish.

Rocky Mountains

Topography and soil—mountainous with some plateaus in the interior; rocky with thin sandy soil.

Watersheds—snow-fed lakes and streams; rapid run off in the spring; swiftly flowing rivers.

Climate and humidity—precipitation as high as 100 inches in the higher areas; extreme variance in temperatures and humidity.

Plant life—Engelmann spruce, lodgepole pine, cedar, hemlock, larch, and poplar.

Wild life—porcupine, hoary marmot, squirrel, rabbit, sheep, goat, moose, deer, panther, and grizzly and black bear; trout, and no birds.

West Coast

Topography and soil—wide fertile river valleys surrounded by mountainous topography.

Watersheds—well drained by rivers flowing into the Pacific which tend to flood during the spring run off.

Climate and humidity—very humid; high rainfall; mild climate; maritime.

Plant life—Douglas fir, western hemlock, western red cedar, and Sitka spruce.

Wild life—porcupine, marmot, rabbit, grouse, mule deer, red deer, and bear; trout, salmon, various cod, and flounder.

Boreal Region

Topography and soil—lies on the Canadian Shield; shallow, poor soil; overlying rock; rolling terrain; hummocky.

Watersheds—extensive muskeg; innumerable lakes; fairly fast flowing streams; most drainage to the north.

Climate and humidity—precipitation variable 10 inches in the west to 10 inches in the east; cold winters; short hot summers.

Plant life—spruce, balsam, white birch, poplar, jack-pine, and tamarack.

Wild life—fish in most lakes and streams; mice, red squirrel, varying hare, porcupine, musk-rat, white tail deer, moose, weasel, mink, marten (fisher), otter, wolverine, fox, wolf, lynx, and black bear; partridge, ruffed grouse, duck, hawk, owl, and eagle.

Northern Transitional

Topography and soil—the same as the Boreal Region except for some permafrost; considerable muskeg.

Watersheds—the same as the Boreal Region.

Climate and humidity—somewhat less precipitation than in the Boreal Region and colder, with shorter summers.

Plant life—scrubby spruce and jack-pine.

Wild life—fish; red squirrel, varying hare, fox, polecat family, and wolf; spruce partridge, ptarmigan, and arctic owl.

Arctic

Topography and soil

(a) Eastern Arctic—high rocky, shallow soil, permafrost, long fiords by the coast;

(b) Mainland barrens—low lying terrain;

(c) Western Arctic—low lying but rolling terrain; and

(d) Arctic Islands—eastern islands mountainous, western islands flat.

Watersheds

(a) Eastern Arctic—glacier-fed rivers which dwindle in summer;

(b) Mainland barrens—extensive muskeg, innumerable shallow lakes, slow shallow rivers;

(c) Western Arctic—few lakes or rivers except north of the mainland barrens.

Climate and humidity—long winters of darkness, surprisingly little snowfall, extreme dry cold; sea frozen from mid October to June; short summers of complete daylight, seldom hotter than 50°F and lasting through July and early August.

Plant life—scrub willow in stream beds and protected places; mosses, lichens, and berries.

Wild life—abundant in fish; lemming, ground squirrel, arctic hare, fox, wolf, polar bear, seal, walrus, whale, caribou and musk-ox; duck, geese, ptarmigan, and sea birds on the coast.

PARACHUTE
JUMPING

CHAPTER 3

PARACHUTE JUMPING

HISTORY

There is some evidence that Chinese acrobats used parachute-like devices in 1306.

Leonardo Da Vinci prepared a sketch and notes for a rigid pyramid-shaped parachute approximately 1500.

Modern parachutes were evolved from the crude canvas devices used to descend from hot air balloons in the late 18th century and during the 19th century.

J. B. Blanchard made the first recorded successful use of a parachute when he dropped a dog in 1785. He, himself, descended safely in 1793.

During the latter part of the Great War, German aviators used the parachute, although it did not prove too successful.

In 1921 the British and Americans experimented with a seat type of parachute, one that could easily be carried by aircrew. To achieve perfection, more than 1,500 trial jumps were carried out.

Proper Fitting of the Harness

The harness is designed to distribute the opening shock evenly throughout the body, if proper fit has been attained. A poorly fitted harness may cause badly wrenched shoulders as well as severe injury to the crotch area.

Ensure that you are properly fitted before you accept your safety harness.

Daily Inspections

Once you have a parachute on loan it is recommended that you carry out the following daily inspections. If, when using these inspections as a guide, your chute, harness, or travelling bag is faulty, return it immediately for repair and reissue or replacement.

(a) Packing Date. A pocket on the underside of the pack contains an inspection slip which indicates the date packed, by whom, and the unit where packed. The packing cycle of all man-carrying parachutes is 60 days.

(b) General Condition of the Pack. When, because of mishandling, the pack is mis-shapen to the extent that operation may be impaired, return it and draw another one.

(c) Acid. An area affected by acid appears lighter in colour and frays readily when scraped with a finger-nail. If any part of your assembly should become contaminated, isolate it immediately and return it as soon as possible.

(d) Grease, Oil, and Dirt. Return equipment as soon as possible if any traces are found.

(e) Tears. Report even the smallest tears.

(f) Rip-cord Pin. Check for corrosion and ensure that the pins are not bent.

(g) Safety Thread. The safety thread acts as a seal and if it is found broken, return the chute immediately.

(h) Bands and Pack Opening. Inspect for condition and security.

Storage

If the following storage procedure is carried out, the chances of (b), (c), (d), and (e) occurring in your assembly will be considerably reduced.

(a) Store in a dry place away from sunlight.

(b) Store in a clean place away from acid, grease, oil, and dirt.

(c) Keep the assembly under lock and key preferably in a metal locker.

NOTE. You are advised to use these storage methods with all your personal equipment—bandoleers, Mae West, etc.

High Altitude Bail-outs

Bail-out at altitudes where oxygen is required presents special hazards as it is necessary to delay opening of the parachute as long as possible to avoid:

(a) loss of consciousness through lack of oxygen;

(b) excessive parachute opening shock; and

(c) frost-bite.

Bail-outs above 30,000 feet require oxygen—a bail-out bottle is a necessity.

Pulling of the rip-cord should be delayed until you are approximately 5,000 to 10,000 feet above the ground level or until you can identify ground features in relief.

NOTE. It takes a body approximately 32 minutes to fall 65,000 feet with a parachute and four minutes to cover the same distance without a parachute.

Stability in Free Fall

There are at least five good reasons for immediate body stabilization after bail-out or after separation from the ejection seat.

(a) The face and body parallel to the earth position eliminates the possibility of body interference with the proper deployment sequence of the parachute.

(b) Orientation with reference to the ground is immediate and continuous.

(c) There is a reduced rate of descent, and therefore, less chance of injuries on deployment.

(d) The limbs-spread face-to-earth position reduces the possibility of violent spinning in either a horizontal or a lateral plane, which can result in confusion and unconsciousness.

(e) If by chance you have failed to hook up your automatic parachute opening device you can in a stable position readily discern whether it is functioning at the proper altitude. Any aircrew member with a few hours air time can immediately tell the difference between 15,000 and 5,000 feet.

Attaining Stable Position

Immediately after separation from the ejection seat the arms should be spread out at an angle slightly ahead and above the shoulders and at the same time the legs spread as far apart as possible, the head held back, and a strong arch in the back.

NOTE. Bending forward at the waist causes a back to earth position.

If spinning takes place, it can be corrected by drawing the arms in parallel to the sides or by assuming a "full tuck" position then slowly re-spreading the arms. This spread position should be maintained throughout the free fall.

Body Position During Rip-cord Pull

In the stable spread position your rate of descent will be approximately 100 mph. and you are in the ideal position for an automatic deployment of the parachute.

If you are operating the parachute manually, simply look at the rip-cord, grasp it with your right hand, and at the same time place your left arm across your waist. Then while pulling the rip-cord from its housing, bring your legs together and hold your chin down.

If you free fall in a closed position your rate of descent can be as high as 260 mph at higher altitudes and 150 mph at lower altitudes.

Handling of the Open Chute

Canopy Check. When your chute has blossomed look up at the canopy to check for tears or lineovers. If you detect numerous holes in the canopy your rate of descent will be much faster and you can expect a harder landing. In case of a lineover, where one or more lines are caught over the canopy, your rate of descent will increase considerably. At the same time you will not have too much control over your parachute. If your rigging lines are twisted you can speed up the unwinding by kicking against the twist. Then carry on with the following procedure.

Orientation. While you still have altitude check the surrounding terrain for habitation, lakes, rivers, or anything that may assist you in survival.

Check Drift. Sight between your feet. This is necessary if you wish to have a proper landing position. Ascertain your altitude by looking ahead at a 45 degree angle. On a sunny day watch your shadow. Never look directly at the ground when approaching it. Your tendency to reach for the ground will straighten your legs thus increasing your chances of injury.

Oscillation (swinging back and forth). This can be reduced with a steady pull on one riser or two or three of the lines.

Planing. For chutes with four risers, to plane forward pull on the two front risers. To reduce forward drift pull down on the rear risers. For planing right pull on the right risers, and for planing left on the left ones. For chutes with two risers, unless you can grasp the shroud lines, you will be limited to right and left planes only.

Para-landing Techniques

When nearing the ground, assume the proper landing position. By this time you should have checked your drift, dampened oscillation, and carried out any necessary planing.

The following are the correct positions for various types of terrain.

(a) Open Terrain

    (i) chin on chest,

    (ii) back rounded,

    (iii) hands on risers, elbows forward,

    (iv) knees slightly bent,

    (v) turn feet off at a 45 degree angle, as taught,

    (vi) present the balls of your feet to the ground,

    (vii) go into your roll, as taught, and

    (viii) spill your chute by running around it or by pulling in two or tnree of the lines which are closest to the ground.

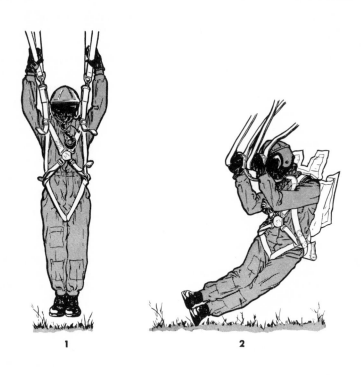

Landing Sequence for Open Terrain. Illustrating body positions for distributing the impact shock equally over the body to cut down the possibility of injuries during landing.

(b) Bush. When landing in wooded areas, carry out the same procedure with the exception that you must protect your face with your arms and have more bend in your knees. Above all keep your feet together.

(c) Water. Do not attempt to judge your height when approaching open water

(i) turn tne quick release box so that the red mark is in the up position,

(ii) place your hands over the quick release box, ready to depress it,

(iii) keep your legs together and your head erect,

(iv) when your feet come into contact with the water (and not before) press the quick release, clear your leg straps, and swim away from the chute,

(v) inflate your Mae West, and

(vi) inflate your dinghy and get into it.

NOTE. The inflation of the life jacket just prior to water entry, particularly for non-swimmers, is recommended. If this practice is followed, the oral inflation valve should be unlocked to facilitate bleeding off excess air in case the pressure between body and harness becomes too great.

Supply Dropping

When you are expecting a supply drop, help the drop crew out by placing proper signals in a clearing where they can readily be spotted from the air.

You can spill these chutes by pulling the apex into the wind or by grabbing one or two lines at shoulder height and dragging the chute into the wind.

FIRST AID

CHAPTER 4

FIRST AID

GENERAL

Definition

First aid is immediate assistance rendered to the injured or suddenly ill person in the absence of adequate medical care.

Purpose

To prolong life, to preserve existence and vitality, and to prevent further injury.

General Rules

Check bleeding and breathing.

Do not get excited but act quickly after you decide which of the injuries needs attention first.

Do not move the patient unless he is certain to benefit as a result.

Keep the patient comfortable and warm; reassure him and avoid having him see his injuries if possible.

Do not touch open wounds or burns with your fingers or other objects.

Do not give unconscious patients liquids.

SHOCK

Definition

Shock is a condition which is caused by the loss of an effective volume of blood circulating in the patient's blood vessels. It may be caused by different factors, such as:

    (a) actual loss of blood from wounds;
    (b) loss into the tissues such as in a broken thigh — as much as two quarts may pool in the fractured leg;
    (c) internal bleeding into body cavities;
    (d) loss of other fluids such as serum and plasma in burns; and
    (e) massive loss of fluid through sweating, vomiting, and diarrhoea.

Signs of Shock

The skin is pale, cold, and clammy, the pulse is fast and weak, and the breathing is fast and shallow.

Treatment of Shock

Control bleeding:

(a) external signs
   (i) arterial—bright red—spurting,
   (ii) venous—dark red—rapid flowing, and
   (iii) capillary—steady oozing; and

(b) internal signs
   (i) lungs—chest pains—bright frothy blood from the mouth, and
   (ii) abdomen—stomach injury—vomiting blood of coffee ground colour.

Stop bleeding by a pressure bandage at the site. Complete rest is essential.

Facilitate or restore breathing:

(a) by artificial respiration; or
(b) by giving oxygen if the aircraft supply is available.

Control pain. Sever pain must be relieved. Pain can often be eased by keeping an injured person quiet and warm, carefully changing his position to keep him comfortable, splinting an injured arm or leg, and handling him gently at all times. Give 222s in accordance with instructions when a severely injured person, suffering acute pain, has to be transferred to a safer location, or when severe pain cannot be controlled by any other means. Never give them to a patient who is unconscious or sleeping, who has a severe head injury, or whose rate of breathing is twelve respirations or less a minute.

Prevent additional injury:

(a) protect the injury;
(b) splint any fractures before moving; and
(c) handle gently.

Replace fluids. Give hot sweetened drinks.

Prevent exposure:

(a) protect under the patient as well as on top; and
(b) do not overheat.

The head should be lower than the feet.

Reassure the Patient

WOUNDS

Preliminary Treatment

Expose to determine the extent of the injury.
Stop bleeding:

(a) apply a firm pressure dressing and in extreme bleeding cases apply a tourniquet (the tourniquet should be used only as a last resort);

(b) if the patient is coughing blood as from a damaged lung, sit him up with his head supported; and

(c) if the patient is vomiting blood as from a damaged stomach, bend his knees, make him as comfortable as possible, and ensure that his air passage is clear.

Protect the wound:

(a) remove foreign bodies from the surface;

(b) do not probe the wound;

(c) apply a sterile dressing;

(d) dress and splint fractures; and

(e) apply hot sterile compresses to combat infection.

Complicated Wounds

Chest wounds. Make the wound air-tight.

Abdominal wounds:

(a) place the patient in a comfortable position;

(b) give nothing by mouth; and

(c) apply a large binder type dressing.

FRACTURES

Indications of Fracture

The following are indications of fracture:

(a) an audible snap;

(b) pain at the site;

(c) loss of power of the affected limb;

(d) deformity;

(e) tenderness;

(f) swelling;

(g) discoloration; and

(h) crepitus.

General treatment:

(a) administer sedatives;

(b) immobilize the fracture and neighboring joints; and

(c) avoid contamination.

Special Fractures

Fracture of the Spine:

(a) Indications. Pain, tenderness, or deformity at the site of the fracture and possible paralysis or loss of sensation below the site of the fracture.

(b) Treatment. Fractures of the spine should be treated with great care because of the danger of injury to the spinal cord. If the back is allowed to hump, the broken bone may cut the spinal cord.

37

Fractured Ribs

(a) Indications. Pain, especially on breathing or coughing. The broken rib is tender and the break can sometimes be felt. The patient usually holds his hand tightly over the break. If the lung is punctured he may cough up bright red frothy blood.

(b) Treatment. Tie a firm bandage round the lower ribs.

Fracture of the Skull

(a) Indications. Unconsciousness, swelling, or laceration of the scalp; bleeding or leakage of spinal fluid from the nose, mouth, or ears; a difference in the size of the pupils or the eyes, blackening of the tissues under the eyes, and paralysis or twitching of the muscles.

(b) Treatment. Treat as for shock. Keep the patient at rest in a semi-prone position.

Fracture of the Lower Jaw.

(a) Indications. There may be pain on movement of the jaw; irregularity of the teeth, inability to talk or swallow in some cases, and bleeding from the mouth.

(b) Treatment. Clear the nose and keep the mouth closed. Immobilize using bandages.

Fracture of the Collar Bone.

(a) Indications. The injured shoulder is at a lower level than the uninjured one. The patient is unable to lift his arm above his shoulder, and he supports the elbow of the involved side with the opposite hand. The fractured ends can usually be felt under the skin.

(b) Treatment. Use a T splint or figure eight bandage with the centre of the eight between the shoulder blades, and small arm sling to support the shoulder on the injured side.

Dislocations, Strains, and Sprains. Damage to ligaments, tendons, and muscles. Treat as for fractures.

BURNS

Burns are extremely painful and the resultant shock is more severe than that encountered in most other injuries.

Treatment:

(a) treat for shock;

(b) give 222s;

(c) avoid contamination of the burned surface;

(d) cover the injury with sterile vaseline impregnated gauze;

(e) over this place a thick layer of sterile gauze dressing or similar sterile padding; and

(f) bandage firmly.

ASPHYXIA

This is unconsciousness from lack of oxygen.

Treatment:

(a) remove the cause or the patient from the cause (protect yourself);
(b) clear air passages, loosen clothing, and remove false teeth;
(c) administer artificial respiration and give oxygen if available;
(d) give no sedatives (depressants) or alcohol; and
(e) treat for shock.

HEAT STROKE — SUN STROKE

The temperature regulating mechanism of the body fails and the body temperature rises to dangerously high levels.

Signs and symptoms of heat stroke:

(a) skin flushed, hot, and dry;
(b) headache;
(c) dizziness;
(d) irritability;
(e) visual disturbances; and
(f) nausea and vomiting.

Treatment:

(a) cool the patient quickly, particularly about the head area;
(b) give salt solutions by mouth; and
(c) give no stimulants.

FROST BITE

Signs and symptoms:

(a) the skin assumes a dull whitish pallor;
(b) there is a feeling of numbness or prickling associated with the formation of ice crystals in the tissues;
(c) with deep freezing the tissues are solid and immovable; and
(d) prolonged exposure to cold causes the person to become numb and drowsy, his eyesight fails, he becomes unconscious, and his respiration may cease.

Treatment

(a) Do not rub.
(b) If the frozen part is on the face, ears, or trunk, cover it with the warm ungloved hand. If a hand is involved, insert it within the shirt, up against the body. If a foot is involved, remove the shoe and sock and place the foot within the shirt and against the body of another man.
(c) Treat as a burn, wrap in sterile dressing, cover warmly, and put at complete rest.
(d) Remove the patient from exposure and give warm drinks, food, and clothing. Artificial respiration, stimulants, and oxygen may be necessary in cases of prolonged exposure.

FOREIGN BODIES

Ears

To dislodge a foreign body from the ear, syringe the ear canal with lukewarm water. Be sure to direct the flow of the water along the side of the canal. If the object does not come out, do not try to dislodge with pins, wire, etc.

Nose

This usually presents no immediate danger. The object can generally be dislodged by stopping the unaffected nostril and blowing the nose. Any attempt to dig the object out will cause more swelling and lodge the object more securely.

Eyes

Do not attempt to remove the foreign object with the fingers or to rub the eye.

(a) Close the eye for a few minutes until the spasm of irritation is over, then grasp the lashes of the upper lid, and raise the lid. Repeat this process a few times. In many cases the object will be washed out by tears.

(b) When this method fails, a search must be made under the lower lid. Place the thumb below the eye and pull down. This exposes the under surface of the lower lid for examination. The foreign body if seen can be picked off with a cotton tipped stick. If the foreign body is not seen, examine the upper lid. Have the patient look down, place a match across the upper lid, and then with the other hand grasp and raise the lashes, turning the lid back over the match. Lift out the foreign body with a cotton tipped stick. Place some eye ointment on the inner surface of the lower lid.

(c) If the object is embedded in the eye or lid or if there is difficulty removing it, close the eye and apply an eye patch held in place by strips of adhesive. Do not use a knife, toothpick, pin, or any similar object to remove foreign bodies from the eye.

INSECT BITES

Mosquitoes, black flies, deer flies, and midges bite. Bees, wasps, and hornets sting.

Treatment

(a) Prevention is the best cure for insect bites. Keep yourself protected at all times with head nets, gloves, light coloured clothing, fly repellents, etc.

(b) Soaking in warm water is the easiest and best all around treatment for bites.

(c) A paste of clay and water will reduce the sting of the pests.

TRIANGLE BANDAGE

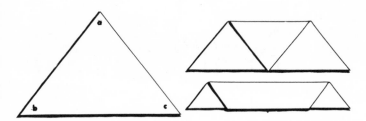

Triangular Bandage Folded as a Cravat

Triangular Bandage Applied to the Head

Triangular Bandage Used as a Sling

41

Hip Bandage

Hand Bandage

Knee Bandage

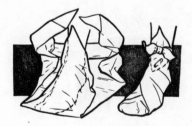

Foot Bandage

Doughnut Bandage
or
Ring Pad

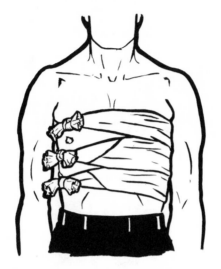

Immobilization of the Chest with Cravats

Fracture of the Humerus Immobilized by Binding to the Chest Wall

43

THE ROLLER BANDAGE

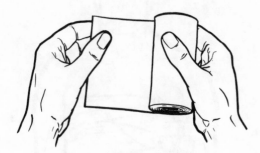

Starting the Roller Bandage
(Hold the roll in the right hand, loose end on the bottom.)

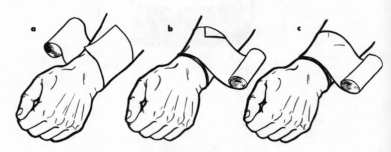

Anchoring the Roller Bandage
(Make a few turns in the same spot.)

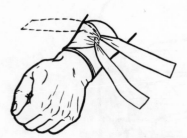

Fastening the Roller or Spiral
Bandage
(Tear the end into two tails, tie a knot, carry one tail in the opposite direction, and tie.)

Simple Spiral Bandage
(Used in bandaging cylindrical parts; overlap each turn one third.)

Figure Eight Bandage for Joints   Spiral Reverse Bandage

(For tapered surfaces—overlap each turn one third.)

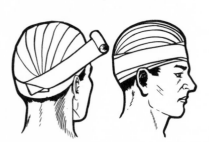 

Recurrent Bandage   Start of the Recurrent Bandage

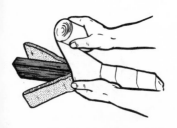 

Padding a Wooden Splint   Applying a Splint

SPLINT FOR FOREARM

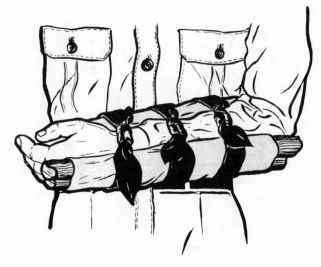

Sticks Rolled in Cloth to Form an Improvised Splint for the Forearm.

Sticks Rolled in Blankets to Form an Improvised Splint for the Leg.

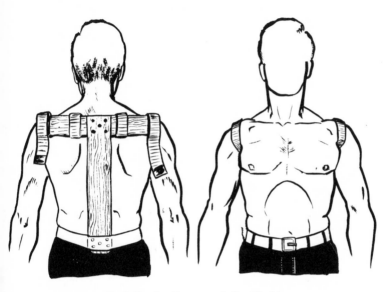

T   Splint for Fracture of the Clavicle.

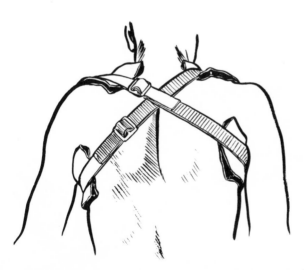

Method of Immobilizing the Clavicle. Use two belts in figure eight fashion.
Pads should be placed over clavicles and under arm-pits beneath belts.

47

SHELTERS

CHAPTER 5

SHELTERS

INTRODUCTION

Once first aid has been administered to the injured it becomes necessary to provide a comfortable form of shelter. There are many types of shelter that are quickly and easily constructed and the selection of the one to build depends on circumstances, such as the availability of materials, season, geographic location, topography, etc. A few of the recommended types of shelters are:

    (a) lean-to;

    (b) suspension tepee;

    (c) cabin or para-cabin;

    (d) natural shelter;

    (e) aircraft; and

    (f) arctic shelters.

The Lean-to

A pole framework is covered with a thatching of parachute silk, evergreen boughs, rushes, heavy grasses, slabs of bark, or split wood planks. When constructing the lean-to, find two trees seven to nine feet apart with fairly level, firm ground between them. The distance between the trees will be the length of the opening of the lean-to, although it is possible to incorporate variations. The number of people requiring shelter should determine the size. When constructed for one man it should be made long enough for him to sleep across the open mouth of the shelter, whereas for more than one it should be planned for them to sleep lengthwise. One or both ends of the ridge pole may be supported by a pole bipod or tripod instead of utilizing standing trees. This leaves the builder a wider choice of sites. It should be remembered that the steeper the slope angle of the roof the better it will shed precipitation and reflect heat from the fire. A 45 degree slope angle is generally considered a suitable compromise between available interior space and rain shedding effectiveness.

Once the framework has been constructed, proceed with the covering. Spruce boughs make an excellent natural covering, although the branches of any coniferous and of many deciduous trees will do. They are placed on the lean-to in the same manner as shingles on a roof, the first row at the bottom. The brush ends of the boughs are placed down, overlapping the butt ends of the previous row. This method of thatching ensures that rain will be shed more readily. Continue to lay rows of boughs in this fashion until the top or back roof of the lean-to is covered. Then repeat the thatching procedure until the entire roof is covered to a depth of at least six inches. The triangular sides are filled in with large boughs set butt end up as in thatching.

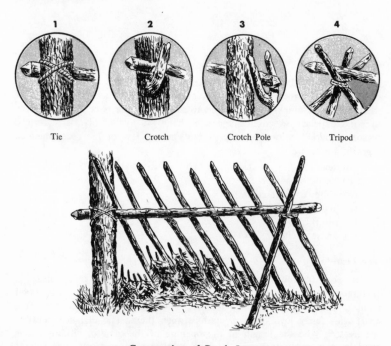

1	2	3	4
Tie	Crotch	Crotch Pole	Tripod

Construction of Brush Lean-to

Parachute silk or wing covers provide excellent lean-to covering and can be used either in lieu of or in conjunction with evergreen boughs. If the temperature is very low, place the fabric on the framework first, and then thatch with boughs on top. The light colored cloth on the inside of the shelter will reflect the heat from the fire and provide greater warmth. If there are heavy rains or melting snow, put the boughs on the framework first and the cloth on the top. This will aid in keeping the shelter dry. If available, a double layer of fabric is advisable.

Lean-to

The lean-to is an excellent shelter even in winter since it permits the utilization of any desired type of fire. With a low mouth, a depth no greater than the width of a sleeping bag, and the full length of the body exposed to the fire, a person can be surprisingly confortable in the coldest of weather. It is possible to build a shelter of this type to house several people, but it is not nearly as comfortable sleeping with either head or feet to the fire as it is sleeping crossways. Two lean-tos may be constructed facing each other to share a common fire but it is difficult to arrange the shelters to avoid drawing smoke back into one or the other of them. You may succeed at first only to find that a slight wind sets up eddies which make the smoke unbearable. Two lean-tos facing each other and joined at the top will make a pup tent.

The Suspension Tepee

This is a simple quickly erected tepee. Cut the shroud lines of your parachute about two feet from the periphery, tie a rope or piece of shroud line around the cords in the apex of the chute, and throw the rope over an extended limb of a tree, a crossbar between two trees, or the apex of a tripod made from poles of at least fifteen feet in length. This done, secure the canopy at the desired height and stake out the periphery with pegs, rocks, or sod, thus forming a conical tent. The circumference of the tent will be determined by the number of inhabitants and in most cases several gores of silk will be surplus. If there is a need for additional silk for other purposes, these extra gores may be cut out, or they may be left loose to form the entrance.

If it is planned to build a fire in the shelter, it is necessary to provide an adequate vent before elevating the canopy. In wooded areas, where winds are generally not strong, the hole in the apex is too small for proper ventilation and it is necessary to slit the canopy a few inches down along the centre channel of a gore seam. Keep the vent hole open by tying in a cross of sticks the desired opening size. Build the fire in the centre of the tepee, directly under the vent hole.

Smoke-filled Tepee

When mosquitoes, black flies, and other insects are numerous, a smoke-filled tepee may prove to be less objectionable than the blood-thirsty myriads outside.

Suspension Tepee

Another type of tepee, similar to that used by the Plains Indians, is shown below.

Centre Tree

Cabin or Para-cabin

This shelter requires a considerable amount of work and when completed will have a degree of permanency that the previously mentioned shelters do not have. When building a cabin, particular attention should be paid to the choice of location, since the cabin will not be portable. Choose an area close to a water supply, yet not in a valley. The ridges offer much more comfortable living conditions, freedom from insects, and so on. The area chosen should also offer an abundant supply of long straight logs, four to eight inches in diameter. The simplest method of construction is to build four walls log cabin fashion to a height of about three feet and then build a framework of light poles to support a covering of parachute material.

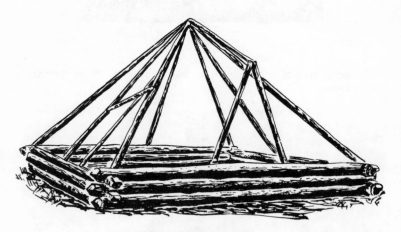

Para-cabin Framework

From this stage it is a simple matter to take a parachute and place it over the framework with the apex of the chute at the top of the roof, to form a finished shelter. It is preferable to employ a double layer of fabric with an air space between, when possible, to improve the insulating and water shedding qualities of the roof.

56

Para-cabin

To build a cabin without the use of parachute material it is necessary to construct the walls to the desired height and to add a sod or thatched roof. Do not make any attempt to build an elaborate gable roof. A flat roof with a slope to the rear is all that is required. The lower the roof, the easier it is to heat the cabin.

This type of shelter requires some form of stove for cooking and heating as the ventilation will not be sufficient for an open fire under normal conditions.

Natural Shelters

Caves may be encountered, particularly in hilly or mountainous areas and by the shores of rivers, lakes, and seas. Caves should not be overlooked as potential shelters but one must remember that caves are frequently damp and are sometimes already occupied. The base of a large overhanging rock will sometimes provide sufficient protection from the elements.

A reasonably large, fallen tree, if lying in a secure position, can be cleared out underneath and closed in by laying boughs or some other siding material over the protruding branches. Care should be taken that branches on the underside of the fallen tree, which may be keeping it off the ground, are not removed. The base of a large tree with thick low branches can also be used.

Aircraft

In warm weather, the aircraft fuselage, if sufficiently intact, and portions of the wing and tail can be made into a comfortable shelter. The main consideration will be the danger of spilled gas and fumes. The aircraft fuselage does not make a good shelter during winter because the metal will conduct what little heat is generated away from the shelter. If emergency tents can be salvaged from the wreck, then the survivor needs only to pick a good location.

Arctic Shelters

Tools. The combination snow saw-knife in your survival kit or a snow knife is essential to survival north of the tree line. With it you can cut snow blocks to build yourself a shelter.

Snow Saw-Knife

Material. The snow from which the snow house is built is in a firmly packed and frozen form which has several characteristics not often encountered south of the tree line. It is solid enough that a cubic foot block will support the weight of a man, yet it can be cut, sawed, or split with ease. Even in the Arctic only a small percentage of the snow is suitable for snow house building. First look around for an area where snow-drifts are deep enough to permit cutting snow blocks from a vertical face. This will require a depth of nearly two feet. The snow should be firm enough to support your weight with only slight marking by footprints. Probe into the snow with your saw-knife or a long quarter-inch rod. Try to find a place where the resistance to the probe indicates an even firm structure, free of harder or softer layers. When you find a spot, probe around to ascertain whether enough good snow is available. It is well worth hunting for an hour to find proper snow as you will save the time during snow house building. If snow of sufficient depth to cut vertical blocks cannot be found it will be necessary to cut them from the flat surface of the snow. This is time consuming and requires a much larger area of snow, and the snow house will have to be built higher, beause it cannot be dug into the drift.

The Fighter Trench

If time does not permit building an igloo, the survivor should for the first night erect a fighter trench. It can be built easily and quickly with minimum work for the result achieved.

If a large drift of snow at least three feet deep is available, the shelter can be made by cutting large vertical blocks from a trench just wider than the sleeping bag and long enough to accommodate the one or two builders. The snow blocks are stood on each side of the trench.

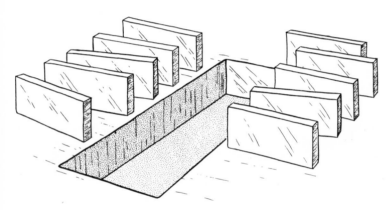

Cutting the Snow Blocks

When the trench is completed a notch is cut along each side to provide non-slip support for the snow block roof.

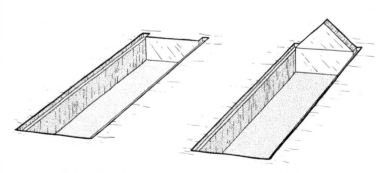

The End Block   The Trench

A triangular block is placed at one end of the trench as a support for the first snow block of the roof.

59

The first roofing snow block is out shorter than the others, in order that the succeeding blocks will overlap, each supporting the next.

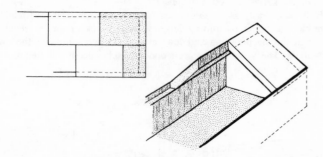

Commencing the Roof

The remainder of the roof blocks are placed in a similar manner. In a two man trench an entrance door is placed halfway down the trench, opening into a roofed over square pit which allows room for cooking and removing clothing before entering the sleeping bag. Be sure to cut a ventilating hole in the roof and have a good snow block handy to close the entrance at night. If snow depth permits, a pit or "cold well" should be dug out just inside the entrance to provide a lower heat level. This will also ease the problem of dressing and undressing.

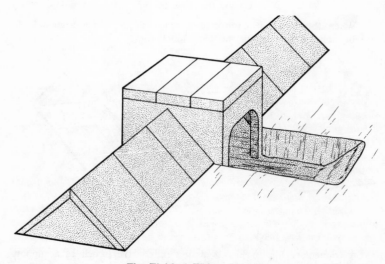

The Finished Fighter Trench

If no deep snow drifts can be found, a trench style shelter can be erected by building a wall of blocks enclosing the shelter area. This wall is then roofed over with large slabs which are hollowed slightly on the inside, after erection, to form an arch.

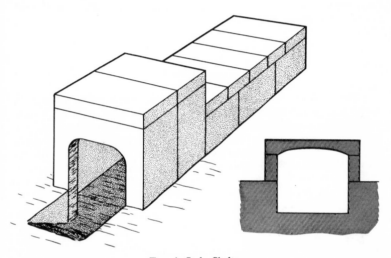

Trench Style Shelter

The fighter trench while a good emergency shelter is too cramped to permit much movement without dislodging the frost on your clothing and sleeping bag, and in time you will become damp without a good means of drying out. This is why you should begin your igloo as soon as you can.

The Igloo

The word "igloo" is of Eskimo origin, and in that language it is a general word for "house" or "shelter". In this manual it will be used to mean the domed snow house, similar to that used by some Eskimo groups particularly in the central Arctic.

The Eskimo igloo is the ideal winter shelter in the Arctic. It is solid, sound-proof, and wind resistant, and it is large enough for comfort. There are a few building techniques which must be mastered but no one of these is particularly difficult. Once the method is learned, the igloo will almost invariably be the shelter used in an emergency.

When you have found a good snow-drift, lay out the floor plan. The Eskimo does this by eye, but he has had a lot of practice. Draw a circle centred on the best snow, with the approximate diameter as follows:

One man	—	8 feet
Two man	—	9 feet
Three man	—	10 feet
Four man	—	12 feet
Five man	—	13 feet

Now, begin to lay in a supply of snow blocks. Cut them from the face of a trench, laid out as shown.

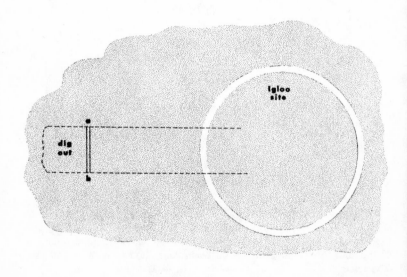

Begin cutting blocks by digging out a clear vertical face at A–B, with a width of about 46 inches and a depth of about 20 inches. Smaller blocks are not much easier to cut, and igloo construction is slower and more difficult with them.

With your snow saw-knife, cut a slot at each end of the block, about two inches wide and the full depth of the block.

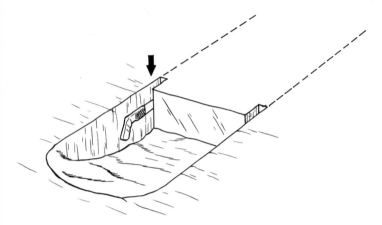

Shaping the Block

Now undercut the block.

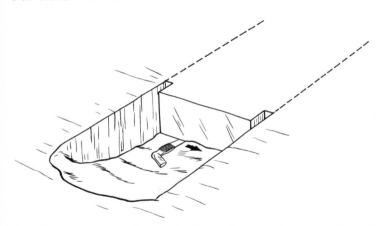

Undercutting the block

Next, score a groove parallel to the face, marking off a block about six inches thick.

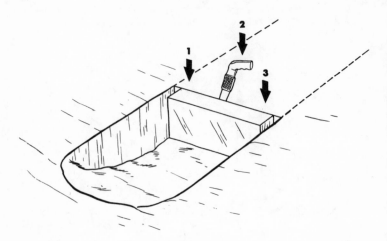

Cutting Out the Block

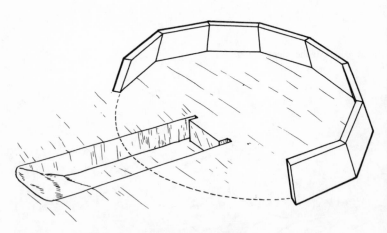

Commencing to Build

If you have a snow saw-knife saw along this mark, breaking off the block with a firm jab in the centre. If you are using a snow knife, deepen the groove by running the point back and forth, then three or four gentle stabs and a firm central stroke will break it off.

Lift the snow block to one side and begin another. When you have about a dozen cut, then you may begin to build.

When the first row reaches the snow block trench, a snow block is replaced in it to permit the wall to be taken across it.

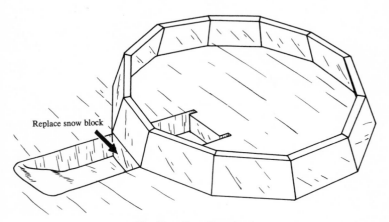

The First Row Completed

Note the slope of the first row of blocks. All end joints are fitted with faces radial to the igloo centre.

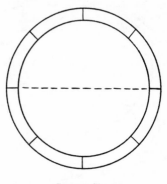

Correct Slope

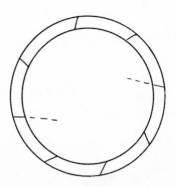

Incorrect Slope

Don't make this mistake, or you are heading for trouble.

When the first row is finished, begin the spiral which will end at the key block. If you are right handed, cut away any three blocks diagonally, sloping down from left to right.

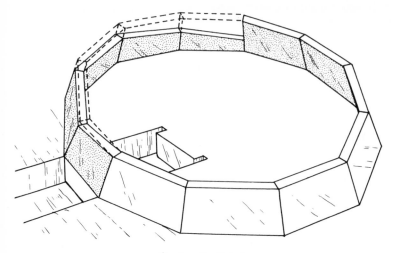

Carving the Spiral

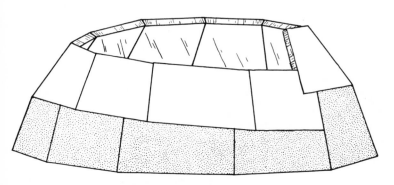

Commencing the Second Row

If you are a southpaw, cut the slope the other way.

Now fit the next block, leaning it inward so that its inner face is roughly tangential to the dome.

Even at this early stage, the block might fall in, except that it is supported by the face of the notch and the top of the previous blocks.

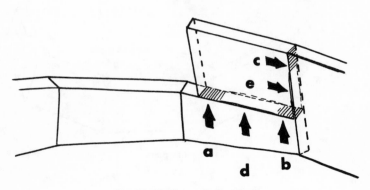

Bearing Surfaces of the Block

The block must bear only at areas A, B, and C. It should not bear at D or E or it will pivot and slip. All blocks from this point on, until the key block, are set in this manner.

Continue cutting blocks from within the igloo circle, fitting them as you go. Don't use blocks less than three feet long or eighteen inches wide if you can help it. Lay small blocks aside for later use in snow bench and doorway building. The slope of the block, which of course governs the shape of the igloo, is estimated by eye. The block is raised into place and the joints are trimmed until the block settles into position.

When the third row is under construction, the slope will be great enough to make careful fitting essential. Each block bears in the same three positions only. The remainder of the joint can gape wide, or almost touch, but these three faces must carry the load to jam in the block.

68

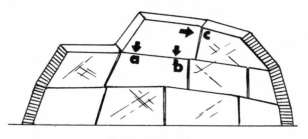

Section Inside Igloo

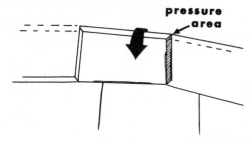

Inward Pressure

The tendency to rotate inward around A–B is resisted by pressure between the upper third of the faces of the new block and the previous block. This face must be radial to the igloo centre, or the previous block may be displaced.

When fitting snow blocks on the A–B–C method described, the block should be lifted into position and the joint fitted roughly, with the faces in contact and the block supported by the left hand. If the snow saw-knife is run between the new block and the previous one and the kerf pushed closed, then a slight undercut on the under face at the end nearest the previous block will leave the joint supported at A and C only.

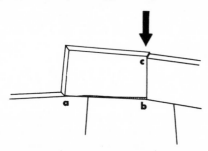

Inward Pressure Bearing Surfaces

69

A firm tap downward at C as shown by the arrow will drive the block into final position, seating at A, B, and C, when it need no longer be supported.

Carry on building, block by block. You will find that the increasing slope of the igloo wall will of course increase the tendency for the block to fall in, but this is compensated by the increasing angle between the A—B axis of the successive blocks as the diameter of the opening decreases. Building actually becomes easier toward the finish, as the blocks will jam firmly into place.

When you run out of snow block snow inside the igloo, cautiously cut a small door as far down the wall as you can, tunnelling underneath to make enough space for the outside workers to push in more building blocks.

Try to keep the curve of the walls symmetrical and avoid a pointed igloo, because the high ceiling would reach the limiting warmth before the sleeping bench gets its share of heat.

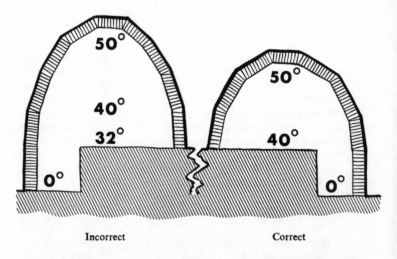

Incorrect   Correct

It is surprising how flat an arch can be built, using the spiral technique. The last few blocks will be almost horizontal, but if you remember the A—B—C fit, they won't fall.

When the remaining hole in the roof is small enough to permit doing so, a key block is fitted. After what you have been doing, this is easy. The edges of the hole should be bevelled at about 15 degrees from the vertical.

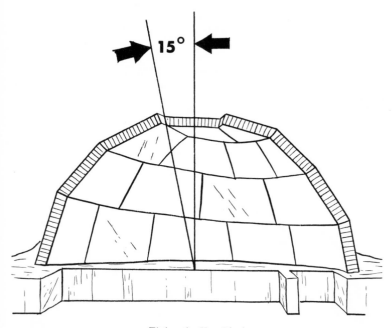

Fitting the Key Block

The hole should be longer than it is wide, to permit passing the key block up through, then juggling it into position. This is tricky, but no one ever seems to fail. By judicious use of your snow knife, cut away the block, letting it settle slowly into position. You have built your igloo!

Making the Igloo Habitable

Across the floor, about one third of the way back from the door, build a snow wall about 20 inches high to conserve warmth.

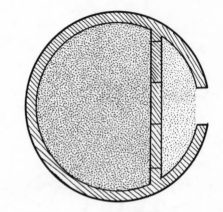

The Snow Wall

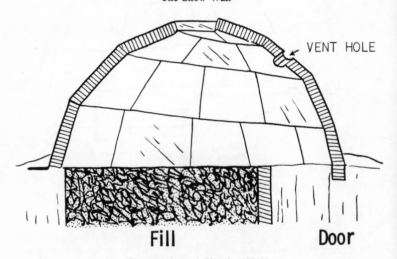

Cross-section of Sleeping Shelf

This will form the front of your sleeping shelf, which will raise you into the warm air trapped above the door.

Shove all the loose snow in the igloo behind the wall to form the shelf. Break up lumps and blocks to soften the bench and to provide better insulation. Level the bench top carefully.

At each side of the door leave or erect little benches allowing about 20 inches of leg room between the sleeping shelf and bench.

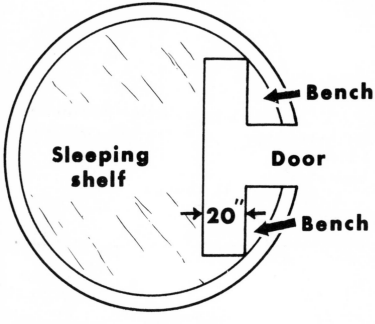

Plan View of Igloo

This is the kitchen and heating area. It must be reasonably close to the bench to permit the cook and lamp tender to reach it without rising from the sleeping bench.

Chink the dome of the igloo carefully with powder snow, which when packed firmly into the open seams will soon harden and stop loss of warm air from the igloo. If you plan a short stay, chink only the outer seams, but for a better job do both inside and outside joints.

You may throw loose powdery snow on top of the igloo to act as chinking, but not so much as to add to the weight of the roof.

You may bank the bottom row of blocks to prevent wind driven snow from causing erosion.

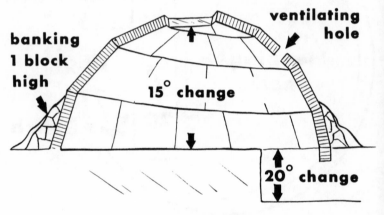

banking
1 block
high

ventilating
hole

15° change

20° change

Igloo Cross-section

If a high wind is blowing, the drifting snow can erode the wall of the igloo very rapidly. A snow wall should be erected to act as a wind-break, and any broken blocks can be piled against the windward wall to protect it from the cutting effect of the drift.

Now, with the igloo chinked, the door cut in and the sleeping bench completed, all you need to do before moving in is to clear out all loose snow. The bench is first covered with caribou skins (or other insulation) and the sleeping bags are then unrolled and placed, heads to the entrance, side by side.

All snow and frost must be removed from hides, bedding, and clothing before they are placed on the sleeping bench.

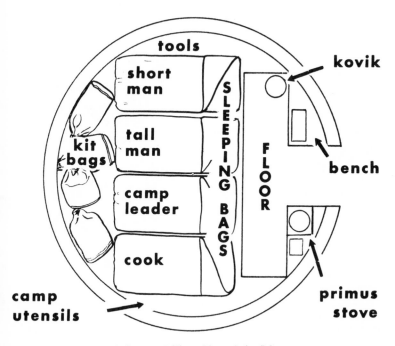

A Suggested Floor Plan of the Igloo

Pots can be suspended from pegs driven firmly into the walls above the fat lamp (koodlik) or the primus stove.

Drying racks made by forcing sticks into the walls above the heat sources will serve the following purposes.

(a) Drying of clothing from which all snow, ice, and frost have first been scraped. Never melt snow on garments—always scrape it off.

(b) Thawing of frozen rations which do not need cooking. This requires quite a long time.

(c) Protection of the igloo wall and roof from melting.

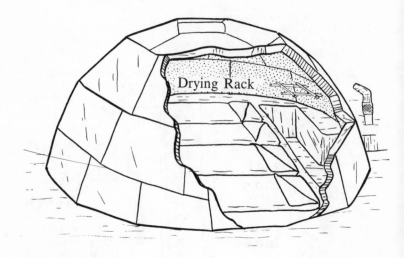

Drying Rack

Persons entering the igloo for a stay of longer than an hour or so, after removing mukluks and snow from garments, should get up on the sleeping bench, out of the way.

The cook, usually at the right-hand bench, has the primus stove, under which is a piece of cardboard from a ration box to prevent it from melting into the shelf and tipping. He may also have a koodlik, if fat is available, for slow cooking.

One man should be responsible for adequate ventilation—keeping the vent holes in the dome and door open enough to avoid risk without freezing the occupants. Carbon monoxide is insidious and dangerous.

During the day the door is left open. At night it is closed by a snow block which should be chinked and a ventilation hole should be bored through the upper part. The more fumes being generated, the larger must be the aperture. Don't wait until the lamp won't burn properly and you begin to feel groggy before letting in air. It is dangerous, and it isn't necessary at all. If the roof hole does not draw properly because of wind, a snow chimney can be made by setting a perforated block over the hole.

The left-hand men remain on the bench, assisting in cooking and maintaining their koodlik. If this lamp is burning animal fat it requires only moderate attention. Lubricating oil is not so easily used, as the flame smokes easily and the wick needs more frequent attention. A little animal fat dissolved in the lubricating oil makes a big improvement in the flame.

If the group finds the igloo cluttered with odds and ends not needed at the moment, a miniature igloo can be built against the outside wall, and a doorway cut through to form a cache. Keep the entrance low to avoid loss of heat.

Now that you are in residence, the igloo will warm up rapidly. If the inner walls start to glaze, form ice, and drip, you are overheating. Take corrective action before icing develops; cut down the heat if you must.

Frying, baking, or broiling have no place in igloo living. Boiling and stewing are easier and prove very satisfactory. Canned goods may be heated in the can by bringing them unopened to a boil in a pot of water which completely covers them. Use the pressure cooker or a tightly covered pot to avoid steam.

Never place an unopened can over direct heat! This makes a fine bomb or grenade, and even a fool rarely makes this mistake twice!

Two good meals a day, breakfast and the main meal in the evening, avoid loss of the working day. A snack at noon will not bring activity to a halt for more than an hour or so. Body heat is derived from food intake, so eat all your ration and supplement with fish whenever possible. Eat fats rather than burn them if the supply is low. A diet of meat is good for you, despite some stubborn superstition to the contrary. Vilhjalmur Stefansson lived for a full year on meat alone to prove this point. If you are forced to live solely on the products of the chase, you must eat flesh, fat, liver, and every edible part to ensure that you don't suffer from dietetic deficiencies.

A snow block (Kovik) may be kept on the floor for use as a chamber-pot after the snow block door is closed for the night. The user is responsible for its sanitary disposition.

The Koodlik

The Eskimo fat burning lamp, or koodlik, has provided heat for comfort and cooking for thousands of years, giving a quiet and pleasant light and warmth to the native home. Properly tended it does not smoke or smell, and it can be controlled to give more or less heat on demand. It was carved laboriously from soap-stone in the form of a shallow pan of half-moon shape. The straight edge of the lamp was bevelled to support the wick, made of arctic cotton or moss. Seal oil or caribou fat was used as fuel. To avoid its melting into the snow shelf and to keep it warm enough to render fat, it was supported on short sticks driven into the shelf.

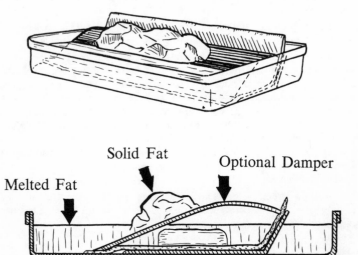

Melted Fat   Solid Fat   Optional Damper

Section Through Tin Can Koodlik

You can improvise a fat lamp out of any flat pan, such as a ration can. If you have fat to burn, all that is required is a piece of heavy cotton, linen cloth, or absorbent cotton for a wick and a sloping ramp to support it. You can burn lubricating oil in a fat lamp, but the flame will smoke more readily, and the wick will have to be trimmed more carefully to keep the flame below the smoking point. When the level of the oil drops, the flame may follow it down the wick, causing further smoking. A simple damper, made of the tin foil from a tallow candle or a piece of sheet metal, will prevent this, and will permit closer control of the flame. A few drops of aircraft fuel used with caution will aid in lighting the wick. Never try to burn a volatile fuel in the koodlik—you would be far too successful, and you might find yourself in trouble. Don't be the first man to burn down an igloo!

SIGNALS

CHAPTER 6

SIGNALS

RADIO SIGNALS

Aircraft

Try the radio as soon as possible. Conserve the battery and be sure all switches are off after use. Power may be had from:

(a) engines;

(b) batteries—in winter, wrap the batteries in a parachute and keep close to a fire to keep from freezing; and

(c) the APU—remove from the aircraft because of the danger of a spark igniting possible gas fumes.

Gibson Girl (AN/CRT3)

It is carried in multi-place aircraft. Follow the instructions on the set. Power is by hand cranking, the unit held between the knees. Frequencies are 500 kcs and 8364 kcs.

On manual, the set transmits only on 500 kcs. On automatic the set transmits six groups of SOS followed by a 20 second tone, and changes automatically from 500 kcs to 8364 kcs every 40 to 50 seconds. On "light" signal must be keyed manually. There is no radio transmission when the switch is at the signal light. The maximum range on 500 kcs is from 200 to 300 miles, on 8364 kcs from 700 to 1,500 miles. The operating times are from 15 to 18 minutes and 45 to 48 minutes after each hour.

SARAH (Search and Rescue and Homing)

A compact, rugged, automatic signal device, it is effective at any time and in any weather and includes a VHF transmitter (beacon) complete with flexible antenna, a transceiver for voice communication, and a battery which will provide a minimum of 20 hours continuous beacon operation under extreme conditions. Continuous voice operation will reduce the battery life to approximately one hour. The assembly weighs only 3½ lbs. and is designed to be carried on the person. It is sometimes included as a component in the life preserver.

To operate, pull the toggle ring on the top of the beacon portion of the transmitter. The beacon operates on a frequency of 243 mcs. Keep the face clear of the beacon unit when pulling the toggle as the antenna springs away from its housing with considerable force, and could cause serious injury to the face and eyes. Once the antenna has been released you are ready to commence transmission. This is done by pulling the pin on the battery, and the toggle on the antenna housing. To stop, replace the pin. Operating times and procedures are clearly marked on the battery. Follow accurately the procedure applicable to your survival situation. Do not expose the battery to low temperature. Keep it inside the clothing in winter.

Keep the antenna vertical for best results. Under normal conditions an aircraft equipped with the special receiver can receive signals up to 70 nm at 10,000 feet. A normal SARAH search will be conducted on a 25 mile "visibility" pattern. It can be carried on day or night and is of course not restricted to visual flight conditions. One search aircraft can cover 30,000 square miles in four hours. Operate the beacon from elevated terrain, reflective surfaces—keeping the antenna vertical. Use voice only when a search aircraft is seen.

PYROTECHNICS

Very Pistol—1½ Inch

This is standard equipment in most military aircraft.

AP Day/Night Signal

This flare has two signals—orange smoke on one end for day and a bright red flare on the other end for night. Coloured smoke should not be used to colour snow unless more than enough smoke is available. Use it only when an aircraft is sighted. The smoke end may be used at night also; just light the smoke in the fire and it will produce a brilliant light. To operate, remove the plastic cap and fracture the seal by twisting the D-ring. Once the seal is fractured a sharp pull on the D-ring will ignite the signal.

T66 Parachute Flares

When fired, a rocket ascends to an altitude of from 1,200 to 1,500 feet. When at maximum altitude, a flare ignites and burns for a period of from 20 to 25 seconds. The flare is suspended by parachute. Operating instructions are clearly printed on the inner container. Follow the directions carefully. Hold the rocket firmly with one hand, pointing the rocket end skyward. A steady pull on the D-ring which is tied to a string will activate the firing mechanism. Remember a firm grip on the rocket and a steady pull on the D-ring. Do not jerk!

Fusees, Railroad Type

To light, remove the end cap under the waterproof tape and strike the flint against head of the fusee. The spike at the other end is to stick into a tree or the ground. It burns 5 to 10 minutes bright red, but will not burn if too wet.

SMOKE AND LIGHT

Fire and Smoke

These are natural signals, easy to use and very useful. Smoke is excellent on clear fairly calm days but works anytime. Fire and smoke will provide 24 hour service.

Miniflare (Projector Pyrotechnic, Hand)

When fired, a single red star type flare ascends to an altitude of approximately 150 feet to 200 feet and burns approximately 5 to 8 seconds.

To operate, retract the thumb piece on the pencil-like projector and engage it in the safe position notch, hold the projector with the open end pointed in a safe direction, and screw the cartridge into the projector.

To fire, hold the projector at arm's length pointing it upwards, then move the thumb piece from the safe position, retract fully, and release.

Signal Fires

Method

(a) In accordance with the diagram, make three signal fires at least 100 feet apart if possible, and grouped in a triangle. Three fires, or signals in groups of three, are international distress calls.

(b) Along a creek bank or ravine, three fires in a line work.

(c) Build signal fires in an open area, a field, marshy ground, or on rafts out on a lake or pond, if possible, and close to your shelter so a quick dash can be made to light them when an aircraft is heard.

(d) Have fires protected from rain and all ready to light with dry feather sticks and splintered kindling in the centre. Place larger sticks around the kindling in tepee fashion and thatch with green boughs or moss. Keep additional fuel, green boughs, moss, and grass handy as emergency insurance.

(e) If you are near the crashed aircraft, rubber and oil from it make good black smoke.

(f) Smoke signal fires can be lit once a day to attract any possible local people in the area—forest ranger, campers, and rescuers, who may see your smoke during the day or fires at night and investigate.

(g) Continuous burning is unnecessary and wasteful on wood and energy.

(h) If a low inversion above keeps the smoke in layers close to the ground, it is generally possible to get the smoke above it by building a larger fire prior to adding the smoke-making material. This applies to thick wooded areas. Find a good clearing away from trees if possible.

(j) If a thin cloud layer exists, night fires will be diffused and not so readily spotted from the air. It is generally a good idea to keep your signal fires going under such conditions anyway.

(k) Always be careful with fire and ensure that precautions are taken against your fires spreading.

Light Signals

Any form of light can be used. Camp fires, flashlights, candles, etc., may be spotted from the air at night. A good trick is to employ light inside a tepee which lights up like a giant Japanese lantern.

Torch Tree

(a) Select an evergreen tree with thick foliage, that is isolated from other trees to minimize the risk of forest fire.

(b) In winter, shake the tree or hammer the base and remove as much snow and ice as possible.

(c) Build a "bird's nest" in the lower branches of the tree using branches of other trees with dry kindling and bark mixed with them.

(d) Around the base of the tree prepare a bonfire—using feather sticks, dry splintered wood, bark, and any combustible material (like gas and oil from the aircraft if available).

(e) This bonfire will burn and ignite the "bird's nest" which helps fire up the whole tree making it a gigantic torch—visible to aircraft and anyone for many miles around.

(f) Prepare this signal in advance and use precautions against getting the kindling wet or spreading fires.

Flash Fire. If gas and oil are available, use only when the aircraft is sighted. Pour the fuel on the ground or saturate pieces of fabric and light them when needed. Take fire precautions.

Heliograph Mirror. A very useful, important, and easy to carry piece of equipment, this device has probably been responsible for effecting more rescues than other methods. It is in nearly all types of survival kits. Follow the instructions on the back of the mirror. It can be seen many miles away on a clear sunny day. If you have no mirror, improvise with a piece of polished metal. The side of a ration can makes a good usable mirror. Carefully cut a cross about 1 inch long in the centre of the sheet with the point of your knife while the metal is lying on a flat surface. At night a flash-light or candle light directed at the heliograph mirror may be effective.

Aldis Lamp. Still carried in some aircraft, it can be operated from the aircraft power supply.

Aircraft Landing Lights. Use these if they are still serviceable.

Aircraft Parts. The aircraft, itself, is an excellent signal. Cut down nearby trees and shrubs that may conceal it from the air. Keep it clear of snow. Shiny pieces of metal from the aircraft laid on the ground will reflect the sun.

SHADOW AND COLOUR SIGNALS

Shadow

Shadow signals are quite effective when built in a clearing and of sufficient size and contrast. In Canada a cross with arms running NE SW and NW SE will catch maximum sun shadow.

Construction

(a) Arctic Winter—snow block wall—line the blocks along the trench from which the snow blocks were cut.

(b) Arctic Summer—sod, stones, sand, or driftwood walls.

(c) Bush Winter—tramped in the snow; lay green bough signals in the snow; or better still stick them in snow and build a wall of brush and boughs around them.

(d) Bush Summer—rock pile signals—dead wood—bush or logs for letters. Use fresh peeled logs and bark or sod blocks.

Colour

In kits are red or orange signalling cloth strips 8 inches by 10 feet which can be pinned to the open ground as an X or other emergency ground-air signal as shown on the plastic emergency parachute cards which most aircrew carry in their wallets. These cloth strips may also be waved from the highest point around if an aircraft is heard. Snow can be coloured with sea marker dye or smoke from an AP Day/Night Signal flare. On water sea marker dye is effective.

SOUND SIGNALS

These can be used to some effect among aircraft crew separated from each other during bail-out and help to guide a ground party to you or to guide a hunter back to camp. Avoid firing three shots unless in trouble or effecting a rescue. Don't waste ammunition. Keep shots regularly spaced and in groups after ten-minute or longer periods. Shouting and whistling may help guide rescuers to you.

INFORMATIVE SIGNALS

Leave a written note for a search party if you leave the crash scene or last camp site and are on the move. Write pertinent facts: date, direction travelling, number and condition of the party, etc. Leave the message in a bottle or can, if possible, and suspended from a tree or tripod or under a rock cairn. A sign visible from the air should be laid out also to give the direction of travel. For yourself and searchers, blaze a trail.
NOTE. Check travel notes for blazing trails and leaving messages.

CONCLUSION

Establishing contact with or attracting the attention of searchers and rescuers should be your main objective as soon as your vital survival needs have been taken care of.

(a) Have your signals all ready and show them effectively.

(b) Prepare as many types of signals as you can at the best possible sites.

(c) Protect signals and equipment from moisture and cold.

(d) Remember that any unusual sign or colour contrast is visible from the air, even a single trail in the snow.

(e) Use pyrotechnics and guns sparingly and with caution—the supply in kits is limited.

(f) Smoke and a mirror are your best signals when no radio is available.

(g) Care for your signalling equipment—learn to use it and be found.

GROUND TO AIR SIGNALS

Use strips of fabric, parachutes, peeled logs, stones, sods, branches in snow. Try to provide maximum contrast. All figures should be at least 40 feet long.

KEY   CODE

1 Require Doctor, Serious Injuries ..   ▬▬

2 Require Medical Supplies ....   ☰

3 Unable to Proceed ....   ✕

4 Require Food and Water ....   Ⴀ

5 Require Firearms and Ammuni-
  tion .... ⌄⌄

6 Require Map and Compass ....   ☐

7 Require Signal Lamp with Battery,
  and Radio ....   ▬ ▬

8 Indicate Direction to Proceed	K
9 Am Proceeding in this Direction ..	→
10 Will Attempt Take-Off	I>
11 Aircraft Seriously Damaged	L⅂
12 Probably Safe to Land Here	△
13 Require Fuel and Oil	L
14 All Well	LL
15 No	N
16 Yes	Y
17 Not Understood	⅃L
18 Require Engineer	W

FIRE METHODS

CHAPTER 7

FIRE METHODS

INTRODUCTION

Fire is one of the survivor's basic needs. With it he can keep warm, cook, dry clothing, and signal for help. No one should fly without having a means of lighting a fire in an emergency.

REQUIREMENTS FOR FIRE MAKING

Spark

The usual sequence for lighting a fire is from spark to tinder to fuel. The spark may be provided in one of the following ways.

(a) Safety matches—these should be carried by all aircrew. Remember to stow a striking strip with the matches if they are packed in a waterproof container. "Strike Anywhere" matches are prohibited in aircraft.

(b) Cigarette lighter—a good source of spark as long as the flint and fuel last.

(c) Flint and steel—an easy and reliable method of fire lighting. If the sparking metal flint on the bottom of the fire tablet case is available, use a knife blade or similar piece of steel to scrape a spark from the flint into a tinder nest of cotton batting, scraped cotton cloth, or scraped paper fluff. A drop or two of gasoline will provide instant flame. If gasoline is not available, be sure that the tinder nest is large enough to ensure that the resultant fire will ignite to the kindling.

(d) Battery—an electric arc can be produced from the aircraft battery to ignite a fuel dampened rag. Don't do this in or near the aircraft!

(e) Pyrotechnics—an excellent source of fire. Caution must be exercised in their use, and you must beware of needless waste. A railroad fuzee or the night end of the AP Day/Night Signal will produce an instant fire.

(f) Magnifying glass—focus the sun's rays on a good tinder. The lens from a camera, binoculars, or reflector gun sight, or any convex lens should aid in fire starting.

Metallic Flint on Fire Tablet Case

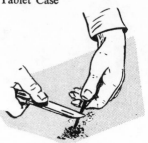

Lighting a Fire

Tinder

The first starter should be fine, dry, highly' flammable material such as:

(a) cotton fuzz;

(b) paper fuzz;

(c) absorbent cotton;

(d) arctic cotton grass tops;

(e) gasoline impregnated rags; or

(f) dry dead grass or witch's hair.

NOTE. Tinder absorbs moisture readily from the atmosphere and may be least effective when you most urgently require it.
Keep Your Tinder Dry!

Feather Stick

Fuel

In going from the tinder to the fuel stage in fire lighting, it must be borne in mind that large fuel materials require greater heat to ignite; therefore, it is essential that some form of kindling be used to nurture the fire until it is hot enough to ignite larger fuel. A few suggested forms of kindling are:

(a) dry, dead, evergreen twigs;

(b) birch bark, shavings, wood chips, or fine splinters of resinous wood;

(c) feather sticks (dry sticks shaved on the sides in a fan shape); or

(d) gasoline or oil impregnated wood.

A good supply of fuel should be gathered prior to attempting to light the tinder in order to maintain the fire. Different types of fuel are desirable for a variety of requirements. Use what is available, bearing in mind that all woods burn better when dry and that pitchy woods or wet woods smoke. The finer the wood is split the less smoky the fire will be. The denser the dry wood, the hotter the fire and usually the slower burning.

Green wood will burn, but requires a hot fire to start. Split green wood fine and start with dry wood.

Ventilation

A fire requires oxygen. Ensure that the fire is well ventilated.

Fire Layout

The ideal camp fire site is on mineral soil or solid rock. Forest fire hazard is always present with fires on muskeg, dry grass, leaves, evergreen needles, or dead roots. A handy water supply or sand is useful for extinguishing flames.

If the ground is dry, scrape down to bare earth. In winter dig down to solid ground, trample the snow, or dig out an area around your shelter and fire area. If the snow is exceptionally deep a small fire may be maintained by lighting it on top of a layer of green logs.

A cooking fire on the trail is ideal if built on a gravel bar, presenting no fire hazard.

Avoid building the fire in a depression because long logs may be bridged up out of the hot coals.

Do not build a fire directly under a tree because of the danger of snow slides or igniting the dry humus and leaves.

A reflector is of little or no value unless it is burning. Large logs rolled on the back of the fire make an excellent burning reflector.

Four common mistakes in fire lighting are:

(a) poor selection of tinder and fuel;

(b) failure to shield the match from the wind;

(c) lighting the fire from downwind (or the leeward) side; and

(d) smothering the newly lit fire with too much fuel, too soon.

Camp Fire Showing the Reflector log principle

Suggestions

Carry ample matches always.

Keep matches dry. If damp, rub them through the hair or back and forth between the palms of the hands with the match head protruding slightly.

Don't waste matches—use sticks from the fire for lighting smokes.

Collect adequate tinder and fuel for the next day and keep them under dry cover.

If the forest is wet use dry standing wood. Split the wood. Make feather sticks for starting the fire.

If you become soaking wet and require an immediate fire there is a danger that water from the clothing will run down and put out the fire, so hold the tinder high to keep it dry.

The pressure stove can be used to light damp kindling.

Pick a fire location sheltered from strong winds.

Beware of using rocks around a fire. Some rocks will explode when heated.

Guard against flying embers. You could lose all your equipment.

Cover your sleeping bag with para fabric or wool at night to prevent sparks from burning the bag.

Bank the fire at night to permit easy lighting from the embers in the morning.

Follow instructions carefully when using pressure stoves. Re-fuel outside, away from open flames. Guard against carbon monoxide build-up.

ARCTIC

There is a lack of natural fuels in the Arctic other than the odd piece of drift-wood or stunted willow, and these are buried in winter. Fuel and stoves must be carried or improvised.

Sources of Fuel

Oil (Engine). In cold weather drain oil from the aircraft before it congeals—on the ground if necessary as it may be used in the solid state. A simple stove or fat lamp may be manufactured as in the diagram. A wick may be improvised from cotton material, surgical gauze, or parts of clothing. Oil should be primed with a few drops of de-icer fluid or gasoline.

Gasoline or Kerosene. The remaining fuel in the tanks will burn in primus stoves or a sand or dirt filled can. Gasoline may be mixed with oil to last longer.

De-icer Fluid. Burn in a simple wick type lamp. A wick is placed through a tight fitting lid.

Candles. Tallow candles are in the emergency kit.

Seal Oil—Blubber. Seal oil or fat of other animals can be used as a fuel. Make a simple fat lamp, using gasoline or de-icer fluid to start rendering fat. (See Arctic Shelters.)

Insect Repellent. A small tray of repellent with a sliver of wood or match stick as a wick will provide some heat. Do not waste repellent in summer.

Petrolatum Gauze Dressings. These are in the first aid kit. Open at the centre, pull up a small piece as a wick, prime with a few drops of insect repellent, and light. After it has burned dry, the wrapper may be used to cook small pieces of meat or fish. Fold the container air-tight. A grill may be manufactured by bending the wire splint in the first aid kit to any desired shape.

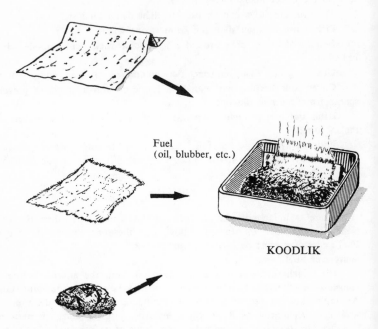

Fuel
(oil, blubber, etc.)

KOODLIK

Bend tin or aluminium and place in the koodlik to support the wick.

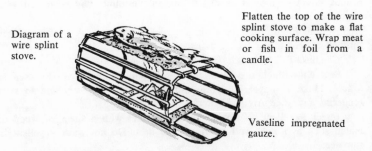

Diagram of a
wire splint
stove.

Flatten the top of the wire
splint stove to make a flat
cooking surface. Wrap meat
or fish in foil from a
candle.

Vaseline impregnated
gauze.

Bend tin or aluminium and place in the koodlik to support the wick.

96

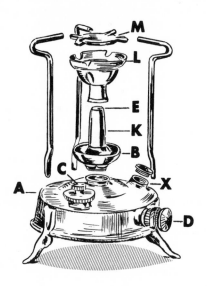

Pressure Stoves

The Primus (model 96) is the standard pressure stove in military survival equipment at the present time. Its component parts are:

A   Filler cap
B   Spirit cup
C   Air valve
D   Pump (with self locking valve)
E   Head opening
K   Head
L   Flame cup
M   Vaporizing plate
X   Plug holder

In assembling, be sure that the head (K) is screwed tightly into the tank.

This stove is built to burn coal oil (paraffin or kerosene) but it functions with many types of liquid fuel. Never fill the stove over three-quarters of its capacity and do so outside the shelter as a precaution against fire. If it is set on a piece of metal or waterproof cloth one avoids wasting any overflow. The head (K) has to be pre-heated in order that the fuel will vaporize to burn properly. This is done by filling the spirit cup with a readily combustible liquid (alcohol, naphtha, gasoline), which is ignited and allowed to burn almost entirely. At this time, the air valve (C) is left open. When the starter fluid is almost expended, close the air valve pump a few strokes (D) and the stove will light. If the starter fluid has burned out before the stove ignites, apply a lighted match at the top of the burner or head (K). If pumping is commenced too soon (before the head is warmed), the stove will flame up. Increase the flame by further pumping: decrease the flame by opening the air valve (C). To extinguish leave the air valve open.

Warning. When fuel, such as naphtha or high octane, is being used, place a shield of cardboard, tin, etc., between the head and the air valve before opening the latter. If this is not done the flame will jump from the head to the escaping fumes at the air valve and this can result in extensive fire and possibly explosion of the stove.

If the flame does not increase after pumping or if the flame is streaky or not atmospheric blue, clean the opening (E) with the needles provided. Keep a lighted match near the head (K) when doing so in order that stove will re-light once the needle is removed. Handle the needle gently, especially in cold weather—it is easily broken. This cleaning process should be done as soon as it is noticed that the flame is not normal—if not, carbon monoxide can build up in an enclosed shelter.

When using the stove for frying, heating a shelter, or drying clothing it is advisable to place a piece of tin or other light metal on the uprights over the flame. This diffuses the heat.

The stove operates and lights best out of a wind or draft.

Carbon monoxide will be formed when insufficient oxygen remains in the air. Maintain ventilation.

HUNTING AND
FISHING

CHAPTER 8

HUNTING AND FISHING

INTRODUCTION

The survivor must conserve and supplement his emergency rations in every way possible, so that he will not starve if rescue is delayed. In Canada this will be best achieved by hunting and fishing. Fish and game are usually available, and if some basic techniques are mastered the survivor can defer use of his survival rations for an indefinite period.

To the majority, hunting implies the use of the gun, but there are other productive methods of taking game. The survivor should plan to use every means at his disposal, favouring those which will require the least effort to achieve satisfactory results.

Snares, traps, gill-nets, and set lines will work for you day and night. Get them into operation as soon as possible. Utilize any available material and improvise. Scout the area of your landing early to learn its game potential. Tackle the job systematically.

Before departing establish a base line or check points by which you can always orient yourself in relation to your camp. This could be a river, a lake shore, a hill, or even a blazed trail north and south of your camp.

The following general rules may prove useful to the hunter.

(a) Walk as quietly as possible.

(b) Move slowly, stop frequently, and listen.

(c) Look around.

(d) Hunt upwind or crosswind whenever possible.

(e) Blend with terrain features as much as possible, i.e., do not stand against the skyline or break from cover without thorough observation.

(f) Be prepared—game frequently startles the hunter or catches him off guard.

Watch for the following.

(a) The animal itself—don't get excited when you see it; very often it isn't sure what you are and will remain still. Make all movements slowly and make the first shot count.

(b) Trails—usually beaten down, through heavy usage. If recently used, trails are excellent for setting snares.

(c) Tracks—may provide a wealth of information, such as: the type, size, age, and sex of the beast; the direction taken; the age of tracks; whether the animal was frightened; and so on.

(d) Droppings—the best indication of what animal has passed; will sometimes reveal favourite roosting spots of birds.

(e) Feeding grounds, water-holes, and salt-licks—good locations for hunting in early morning or evening. Trails leading in to such places may be suitable sites for locating snares or traps.

(f) Dens, holes, and food stores—good spots for setting snares.

SMALL GAME

General

The mainstay of the survivor, particularly if he has no rifle, will probably be small animals and birds. These are well distributed through the Canadian hinterland and may be taken without firearms.

Rabbit

There are several species common in Canada. In woodlands they frequent heavy thickets. They are taken in snares set on their runways, preferably where the width of the runway is restricted by natural or man made obstacles. The balance pole snare and the common rabbit snare are shown in the diagrams.

Close-up of the loop. Wires should be twisted together.

Dead sticks may be inserted into the ground to guide the rabbit into the snare.

a

4½"

3"

Common Rabbit Snare
(Using Wire)

This end should be about 4 lbs. heavier than the other end. Make certain that the balance pole will lift the rabbit clear of the ground.

a

a

Balance Pole Snare
(Using cord)

Nicks to hold up the snare

9" 4½" 3"

Rabbit snares should normally be 4½ inches in diameter and 3 inches from the ground.

103

Squirrels

These are common throughout Canada's forests. They store their food in tree cavities, nests, or holes in the ground but their provender is seldom suitable for human consumption, consisting mainly of pine and spruce cones and the occasional mushroom. The leaning pole snare is a simple and effective method of taking squirrels. It should be employed near their food caches or nests. Three or more snares to a pole are desirable, since squirrels are fond of the company of other squirrels.

Squirrel Snare

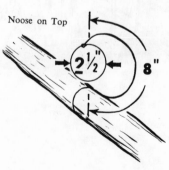

Noose on Top

2½"   8"

Mice and Lemming

These are edible and should not be overlooked by the survivor.

Porcupine

The porcupine is found in most forested areas. Watch for tree with the bark stripped off fairly high above the ground. Its main food is generally bark from trees. It can easily be killed with a club or spear. Be careful in handling—pick it up by a front foot. To skin, open the hide along the belly and peel the hair back over the top of the quills. Work from the inside as much as possible to prevent contact with the quills.

Mink, Marten, and other Carnivorous Fur Bearers

These are not rated as table delicacies but if you can shoot, trap, or snare them put them in the pot.

Musk-rat and Beaver

The musk-rat is found in pond, slough, and marsh areas; the beaver along streams and lakes passing through poplar or willow country (watch for dams). They may be shot while swimming, and the best time is early morning or late evening. Beavers and musk-rats maintain paths and runways where snares can be tried. Any evidence of these creatures coming out from under the ice in the late fall or early spring should be checked; you may cut one off from the safety of the water.

Lynx

Seldom seen, even when they are plentiful, except by hunters employing tracking dogs, the lynx is the most palatable of the carnivores. The meat is not unlike tender, lean young pork.

Fox, Wolf, and Coyote

These are seldom seen except when emboldened by hunger. However their presence is often revealed by their bark or howl. Fox can be captured by a bait snare. In the Arctic, fox can be captured in a baited beehive trap; locate the trap on a high point as the fox usually travels over rather than around hills.

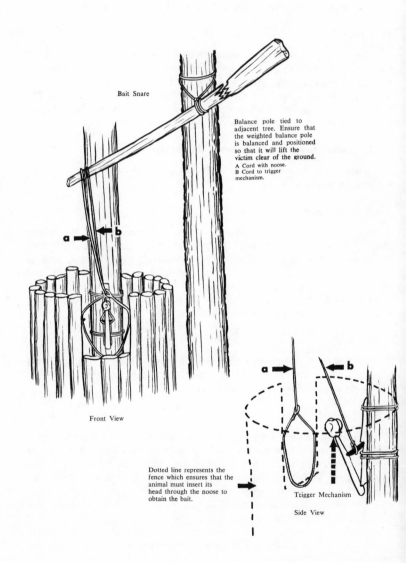

Bait Snare

Balance pole tied to adjacent tree. Ensure that the weighted balance pole is balanced and positioned so that it will lift the victim clear of the ground.
A Cord with noose.
B Cord to trigger mechanism.

a ← b

Front View

Dotted line represents the fence which ensures that the animal must insert its head through the noose to obtain the bait.

a → ← b

Trigger Mechanism

Side View

106

Beehive Trap

Constructed from piled up rocks and stones.

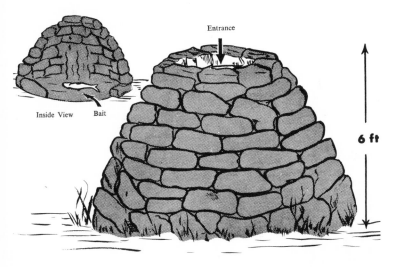

Seal

The Common Jar Seal, found along most of the arctic coastline, is an animal which the survivor may capture and from it obtain food and fuel (blubber). It generally swims underwater and comes up every minute or two to breathe. If frightened it will swim several hundred yards before surfacing. From the end of August to June it will float; hence, if within range it can be shot in the head and retrieved. During the remaining three-month period it will sink, if shot, due to its lean body condition and the decreased salinity of arctic inshore coastal waters at that time. In open water, it is quite curious and will come in close to investigate a scratching or tapping sound.

During the winter the Common Jar Seal lives under the ice and maintains open breathing holes, which are usually covered with snow. These holes are not easily found by the novice, as they are usually located in pressure cracks off points of land. The seal is captured here by waiting without motion until it surfaces and then shooting it in the head or by setting a seal hook at the bottom of the hole (underside of the ice) on which it will catch itself upon diving.

In the spring the Common Jar Seal can be stalked as it suns itself on the ice. It will raise its head every minute or so, and at this time the stalker should remain motionless. If white clothing is not available for camouflage, the stalker should crawl and slither within shooting range.

BIRDS
Upland Game Birds

Grouse and partridge are most often found roosting in thickets, sunning on side slopes, or feeding on the ground, although they are occasionally found in trees, roosting or feeding on buds. Silence in hunting them is not essential. Normally these birds will not fly very far when frightened and, therefore, it is better to flush them out and wait for them to land before shooting.

The spruce grouse in the woods and the ptarmigan in the Arctic frequently remain motionless thereby seeking to avoid detection. This habit often plays them into the hands of even the most ill equipped hunter. They are not difficult to take with a catapult, many are killed by thrown sticks and rocks, and the spruce grouse is easily garrotted, at times, by a wire noose on the end of a pole.

Water Fowl

Birds such as ducks, geese, and coots are normally more difficult to approach than upland game. It is therefore advisable to shoot them on the water, taking into consideration the way the wind and current will take them. If geese are found in their nesting areas during the moulting period, it may be possible to run them to the ground. Do not overlook the eggs or the young. If any waterfowl taken are suspected of being fish eaters, it is advisable to skin rather than pluck them. This, of course, depends upon your tastes which will be influenced by your appetite.

Other Birds

All Canadian birds are edible and most are palatable, but do not expend valuable ammunition for little gain. Gulls will often take a baited hook. An Ojibwa Bird Snare will be quite effective in capturing the Canada Jay (Whiskey Jack or Camp Robber) which will visit most woods camp sites, and a few of them can be made into a stew.

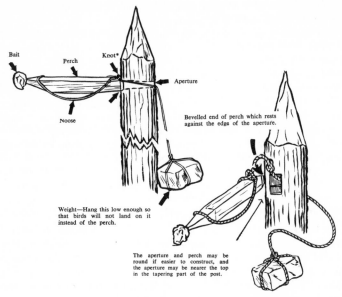

Bait

Perch

Knot*

Aperture

Noose

Bevelled end of perch which rests against the edge of the aperture.

Weight—Hang this low enough so that birds will not land on it instead of the perch.

The aperture and perch may be round if easier to construct, and the aperture may be nearer the top in the tapering part of the post.

*Knot: Retains the perch in position until the landing bird depresses the perch, allowing the weight to pull the knot through the aperture thus trapping the bird by the feet in the noose.

Ojibwa Bird Snare

BIG GAME

General

A big game animal will provide food for a prolonged period, but it will require a suitable gun and some skill, and it normally entails a relatively large expenditure of energy to secure one. If, when scouting the area, you encounter fresh signs of big game you may plan a hunt.

Most big game is abroad at dawn and toward evening. The dawn hunt is best for the survivor. If he loses his bearings, he will have all day to find his way back to camp. If he gets game, he will have daylight to dress it and begin preservation of the meat.

The Deer Family

Deer and moose are found throughout Canada's forest zone while elk and woodland caribou are most common in Western Canada.

In summer, follow ridges overlooking open country, but avoid showing yourself against a skyline. Look for salt-licks and wallows. Flies and ticks torment these beasts during hot weather, and at times their frantic splashing can be heard at a distance. Watch game trails, because most animals prefer to use them when travelling. In winter, the deer, elk, and moose

109

tend to "yard up" in low lying sheltered places, such as cedar swamps, willow clumps, alder swales, or poplar thickets.

When stalking game, hunt upwind or crosswind. Avoid any noise, and stand motionless frequently, scanning the area. Most game is seen while the hunter is standing still. Don't go crashing across country.

Still hunting requires less energy and is often productive. Wait quietly and remain motionless in spots overlooking meadows, game trails, salt-licks, and wallows, preferably crosswind from the area under observation.

If an animal suddenly starts up ahead of you, do not give chase immediately. It may not have known what you are and curiosity may bring it back to check. If you remain motionless and keep watching on all sides, you may get a good opportunity to shoot it. Deer, especially mule deer, do this quite frequently.

Should you wound one of these animals, do not follow it immediately. If it knows it is being followed it may run for miles before it drops, but if you wait five or ten minutes or long enough to smoke a cigarette, it may lie down after a short run and either bleed to death or begin to stiffen up. If you wait too long the animal may regain its wind and depart before you arrive.

Where to Shoot your Big Game

The head or neck area presents a small target unless the animal is close. It may move its head and neck as you shoot.

The heart and lung area is the best shot for most hunters. It is quick and certain, and the animal will not go far.

Typical Target Area When Shooting Big Game

110

The gut region is usually messy but is not to be overlooked if no other shot is available. The wounded animal may travel for miles, leaving no blood trail, before it dies.

When game is taken, bleed, clean, and cool it at once to avoid spoilage.

Snaring

Snares set on well worn trails may save many tedious hours of walking or waiting.

A snare of cable or heavy wire 24 inches in diameter and suspended approximately 18 inches above the ground should produce good results. If the snare is well anchored, the animal will probably kill itself in a short time.

A Method of Snaring Antlered Game

Use a strong, dry pole about 10 feet long and six inches in diameter.

Apache Foot Snare

The Apache foot snare is another effective snare that may produce results when used on a well travelled game trail.

A hole the same diameter as the width of the game trail and about 6 inches deep is dug in the game trail. A rectangular piece of heavy paper or cardboard or thin aircraft skin with a 12-inch cross ($\times$) cut in it is laid over the hole. A snare made of shroud line is placed over the cardboard and fastened to a heavy log. The set should then be camouflaged with light sprinklings of leaves and earth.

The cardboard or paper will ensure that the snare remains on the animal's foot until it is drawn taut. The animal will be able to drag the log until it is exhausted, then it can be caught and killed.

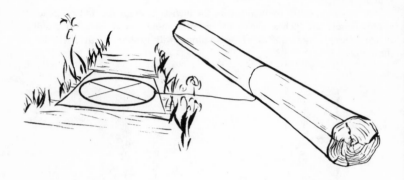

Barren Land Caribou

Once the herd is located, the caribou are usually easy to shoot, particularly when migrating. Approach them low and upwind; even after a shot is fired they will often flank you quite closely to discover what you are. When grazing in small herds, usually in the valley bottoms, they watch the horizon; when hunting them do not top hills quickly in an upright position. Caribou meat is delicious.

Bears

Most bears are not dangerous unless injured or provoked. Bears do become irritable with age, however, particularly grizzly bears, and the survivor who hunts them should be well armed and cautious. Be on guard if you spot cubs as the mother will seldom stray far from her youngsters and she will fiercely resent any intrusion upon her domestic affairs.

Musk-ox

Musk-ox may be encountered on most of the Arctic Islands and portions of the Arctic main land. When danger approaches they face out in a ring around the calves. A gun is required. Approaching extinction, they should not be molested except when in dire need.

Mountain Sheep and Mountain Goat

These are found only at high altitudes. If an opportunity of hunting them is presented, approach them from above. Often these animals are shot but lost through falling from a precipitous location. When skinning mountain goat avoid having the hair touch the meat—it will taint it.

FISHING

Netting

A gill-net is most effective in still water, e.g., a lake (near the inlet and outlet are good locations) or back water in a large stream (for survival don't hesitate to block the stream). Nets can be constructed using the inner cords of parachute shroud lines. The floats on top and the weights on the bottom are to keep the net vertical in the water. When ice is on the lake, the fish are inclined to stay deeper. The smaller the mesh, the smaller the fish you can catch, but a small mesh will still entangle a large fish. A mesh of two and one-half inches is a good standard.

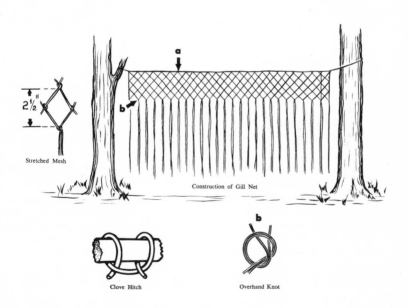

Stretched Mesh

Construction of Gill Net

Clove Hitch

Overhand Knot

113

Here are two methods of setting a net without the help of a raft or boat.

Summer—setting the net out from the shore with the aid of a long pole.

Anchor Line—Pulls the net into place.

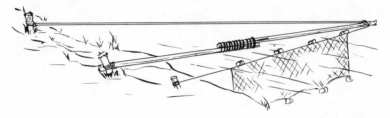

Gill Net Set for Summer Use

Winter—setting the net by cutting holes in the ice on a lake. Ensure the net is set several inches below the ice to prevent it from freezing.

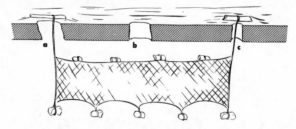

Gill Net Set for Winter Use

With a pole slightly longer than the distance between the holes in the ice, attach a line to one end and, starting at hole A, float the pole to B, to C, and remove from the water at C. Attach the net to the end of the line and pull the net through A until it is set, as shown. Ensure that the line is tied to both ends of the net, to assist in checking and resetting.

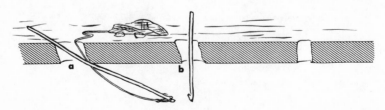

Method of Setting Gill Net Under Ice

114

Spearing

Clear water is a requisite. Refraction can be counteracted by keeping the tip of the spear in the water while waiting. Along the arctic coast the arctic char can be attracted within spear range by bobbing a shiny object up and down in the water.

Snaring

The snare consists of a loop of wire attached to a long pole. The loop is passed over the fish's head and the fish is then jerked from the water.

Hook and Line—Set Lines

This is an effortless method of fishing which does not require the presence of the fisherman. Night lines may be set, using as many baited hooks as possible. Insects, worms, parts of fish (eyes, fins, head, or strips of belly) or whole bloody fish, and red meat are all good baits. One method of selecting a bait is to check the stomach of the first fish caught to discover what it has eaten.

Trolling or Casting

Keep the bait (spinners or wobblers) moving; it attracts the fish more readily. Jigging through the ice is another technique. Here a short stick, a fishing line, and a shiny object near the hook are employed—the last being kept on the move to attract the attention of the fish.

Ice Fishing

115

FOOD AND
WATER

CHAPTER 9

FOOD AND WATER

INTRODUCTION

Food is not, as many people think, an immediate requisite of survival. Man can exist for some time on nothing but water and his own body fat.

The daily caloric requirement of a person varies considerably, depending on age, weight, sex, etc., but is always directly proportional to the amount of energy expended by the body. It is likely that the daily caloric requirement of an average person doing an average job would be somewhere in the neighbourhood of 3,000 calories.

Experiment indicates that a healthy person can subsist for a considerable period of time on 500 calories a day without harmful effects. The aircraft emergency ration pack, when used according to directions, will provide the survivor with approximately 500 calories a day.

Vitamin C cannot be stored by the body but fortunately it is usually obtainable under survival conditions. It usually takes several weeks of improper dieting to bring on scurvy symptoms.

Under conditions of strenuous exertion or cold, additional caloric intake is needed to maintain body temperature. The ration pack is inadequate for this purpose, and food should be supplemented in any way possible. If game is readily obtained it is possible to subsist indefinitely in good health on a diet of meat, fat, and water. When other foods are available, use them in preference to the emergency ration which should be regarded as a last resort.

WATER

Water is more necessary to human existence than food. About one pint (two cups) is considered to be the normal minimal daily requirement. Obtaining good water should present no problem in any of the sparsely settled areas of Canada. There are no known sources of deadly poisonous water. Contamination is normally found only in the vicinity of human habitations, where the practice of survival techniques is seldom required.

119

Do not drink sea-water. It will increase your thirst and may cause further loss of body fluids through diarrhoea and vomiting.

Summer Water Sources

Spring water or fast running water is best but any running water or that from properly drained lakes in isolated areas will be safe.

Standing water of sloughs and muskeg areas can be used with careful bailing. In muskeg areas where the growth is in mounds of varying heights you will often find small pools of good water around the bases of the mounds.

Sometimes when surface water cannot be procured, water can be obtained by digging down into moist soil (usually in the low ground of depressions, gullies, etc.). Muddy water may seep in but it will become clearer if allowed to settle.

Sea-water can be used if a desalter kit is available.

Pools of good snow water can be found on the sea ice in late spring.

Other sources are the sap layer of trees such as birch and maple in spring, dew on plants, and rain-water.

Winter Water Sources

If open water can be found or water obtained through ice, it is to be preferred to ice or snow as no heat is required.

It requires approximately 50 per cent less fuel to obtain a given quantity of water from ice than it does from snow.

A pointed instrument is best for breaking out ice—a number of light taps to start a crack, then one sharp tap to break off a chunk of the size required. On a large surface of a lake or stream, cut toward a crack which is already there in order to avoid getting only splinters and spray.

Icebergs frozen in arctic sea ice are the best source if obtainable. The thin layer of frozen salt water spray outside should be chipped off. There is usually dangerous thin ice or open water around icebergs caused by tides and currents acting on the bulk of the berg which is below the water.

Salt-free sea ice can be found where the ice has summered and frozen in again—usually along the tops of ridges where the salt has leached out. It is bluish with a crystalline structure in comparison with salty ice which is grey and opaque.

Snow which has lain on sea ice for a period of time usually contains salt.

Hard packed snow yields more water than fluffy snow.

If fluffy snow must be used then pack it down into the container. In either case once the container is over heat work the snow with a knife or other such instrument until there is more water on the bottom than will be absorbed by the snow above it. This will prevent the bottom of the container from becoming dry and burning out and also the resulting water from having a burnt taste. Do not eat snow. It tends to dehydrate the body if the snow is excessively cold. If heat is not available melt small quantities in your hand by squeezing and breathing on it before consuming it.

Purification of Water

Boil three to five minutes and shake afterward to restore oxygen and eliminate the flat taste.

Use Halazone tablets as directed.

Use nine drops of iodine a quart.

If there is considerable sediment in water, use filtering or settling processes.

The flavour of safe but unpalatable water may be improved by adding charcoal from the fire and allowing it to stand overnight.

FOOD

Emergency Ration Pack

The carbohydrate ration is recognized as a universal survival ration. It provides the survivor with approximately 500 calories a day.

It is designed to place a maximum amount of the best universal survival ration in the limited space provided in jet cockpits. The term "best universal survival ration" means that the most palatable ration which can be eaten with little or no water and which still produces adequate energy to keep the body alive with few ill effects if a minimum of effort is expended. A glance at the following information should clearly illustrate why the carbohydrate ration has been adopted.

One gram of protein (plus water)	yields approximately four calories of heat energy.
One gram of fat (plus water) but	yields approximately eight calories of heat energy.
One gram of carbohydrate (when assimilated by the body)	yields four calories of heat energy (plus water).

The entire ration should be consumed in accordance with the instructions enclosed in each can. During the first day when no food is taken, energy will be derived from body fat stored from previous eating. It is advisable to do as much of the physical work, such as building shelters, collecting fuel, laying signal fires, etc., as soon as possible during the first day when maximum energy is available.

The ration is mainly carbohydrate, but there is sufficient fat to trigger juices which will counteract the stomach contractions which produce the sensation of hunger. The containers can be used to melt snow or ice, make coffee, etc., and some are provided with wire handles for such purposes.

Commanding officers of flying units have authority to place on their aircraft any foods they wish to have carried for emergency use.

Natural Food

Every effort should be made to discover and obtain natural foods within the crash area before the emergency rations are expended. This search is, of course, going to be in direct ratio to available energy. Naturally the two sources are plant and animal life.

Plant Life

It is difficult to provide comprehensive instruction on plant recognition in a short period of time. Here only the general rules and plants to be definitely avoided will be covered.

Most green plants are a potential source of Vitamin C—rose hips (the buds of the wild rose), tea made by pouring boiling water over labrador tea leaves, spruce tips, willow tips, dandelion leaves, etc.

Anything that is not bitter or anything eaten by birds and animals is probably, but not necessarily, safe to eat. If doubtful, take minute quantities at first and wait 24 hours for a reaction. Gradually increase the quantities, using the same test period, until certain.

Poisonous Plants. There are no poisonous plants north of the tree-line. However south of the tree-line there are three which can be mistaken for edible plants and can cause death.

(a) Water Hemlock. Two to four feet tall, it is the most poisonous plant in Canada. It is a member of the carrot family and has toothed three-part purple streaked leaves which emit a disagreeable odour when crushed and hollow tuberlike roots which emit a parsniplike odour. It could be easily confused with Cow Parsnip which is edible.

Water Hemlock
(Cicuta Mackenziena)

Leaves and
Flowers

Air or Water
Pockets

122

(b) Death Cup Mushroom. This is found in the wooded areas of northern Canada. It is indistinguishable when young but in maturity has a soft white cup-like formation at the base and a broad collar-like ring part way up the stem. Avoid all mushrooms having this structure and also young mushrooms in the button stage. It has been confused with the common edible mushroom by some.

Death Cup Mushroom
(Amanita Phalloides)
(usually 4 to 6 inches
tall when mature)

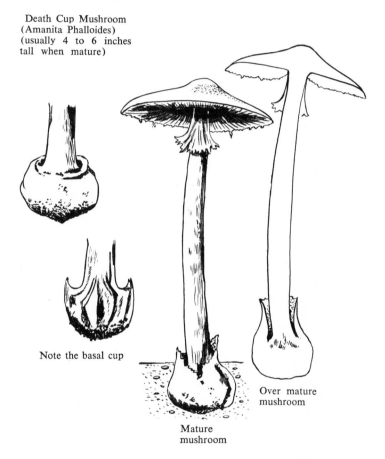

Note the basal cup

Mature
mushroom

Over mature
mushroom

(c) Baneberry. This is a bushy perennial two or three feet tall with small white flowers in a short thick terminal cluster. Red or white berries replace the flowers and resemble dolls' eyes in appearance. The root-stalk is substantial. Avoid berries growing in clusters of this type.

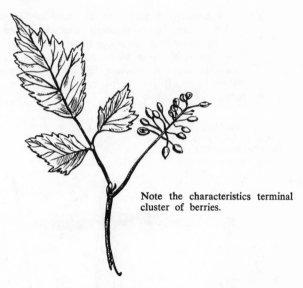

Note the characteristics terminal cluster of berries.

Red or White Baneberry

Edible Plants

(a) Flowers of most plants in Canada are safe to eat either boiled or raw.

(b) Greens such as dandelion leaves will provide roughage and vitamins. These can be eaten raw or stewed. Some delicious edible greens are: bracken fronds or fiddleheads, the lower tender inner twelve inches of cat-tail or bulrush stalks, cow parsnip, young green milkweed pods, young water-lily seed pods, and pigweed.

(c) Roots such as cat-tail, wild carrot, liquorice, etc., will provide starch and protein. Cat-tails are an excellent source of starch since they are found in most parts of Canada and are obtainable in both winter and summer. They are best boiled. Some other common delicious edible roots of Canada are: bracken roots, vetch roots, tiger-lily roots, lady's slipper roots, and the tubers of the arrowhead plant. Water-lily roots and jack-in-the-pulpit roots are edible but must be boiled in two changes of water to remove the acrid flavour.

(d) Berries. The edible berries of this country are too numerous to list here. Blue and black berries not in clusters are generally safe. Red berries are more likely to be unsafe and white berries should be avoided unless positively identified to be safe.

124

(e) Lichens. These are dry scale-like plants, usually found on rocks or old stumps in both the Arctic and woods. They can be boiled and dried, then ground into a powder and stewed for use as a soup thickener, gravy base, and mild seasoning. A common edible lichen of the Boreal Region is the lemon lichen.

(f) Mushrooms. Although some mushrooms are edible, delicious, and filling, they are not particularly high in nourishment and since some are extremely poisonous, they should be left strictly alone unless positively identified as being edible.

(g) Leaves. The leaves of labrador tea, a shrub-like growth found on practically all muskeg areas in Canada, can be steeped to produce an aromatic stimulating beverage. These leaves are boat shaped with a brown pubescent underside. This infusion is quite high in vitamin C.

(h) Trees. Sap from many trees, such as the maple, bass-wood, birch, and poplar, is a source of water with some food value particularly during the spring of the year. At other times the cambium or succulent new growth between the wood and the bark of such common trees as poplar and jack pine can be scraped into a container, this pulpy residue is tasty and nourishing and contains vitamin C.

There are many verses and rules which supposedly differentiate between poisonous and non-poisonous berries and mushrooms but none are completely true. The safest rule is for the survival student to become familiar with a few plants which can be used as variations in diet and a supplement to the emergency rations. The best place to do this is on field trips. Only those who make this a lifetime study can hope to exist satisfactorily for a prolonged period of time on plants alone.

For illustrations of edible plants see Appendix A to this chapter.

Insects

Grasshoppers or locusts are considered to be a delicacy in many countries. It is best to remove the wings and legs and toast the body on a stick. The flavour is not at all objectionable and is said to be nut-like.

Grubs, the white wood burrowing larvae of beetles, are usually found in rotting logs or stumps. Toast or boil them.

Ants are delicious, especially the large black type often found in rotten logs. Remove the head, thorax, and legs and eat. The eggs are edible if enough can be procured but are dry and tasteless.

Snails

Both aquatic and terrestrial snails are an excellent source of nourishment when obtainable.

Earthworms

The large types particularly are eaten in many countries.

Reptiles

Lizards, frogs, snakes, and turtles are all exceptionally tasty whether boiled or fried.

Game—Meat

All Canadian birds and animals are edible except the livers of the polar bear and bearded seal. These have an excessive vitamin A content which produces a toxic reaction.

Dressing Game

Some birds, such as ptarmigan and the various species of grouse, can be skinned using the fingers only. Break the skin on the breastbone and work around the body. Sea birds such as gulls, fish-eating ducks, etc., should normally be skinned to diminish the fishy taste. The craw or first stomach should always be checked as the content is not digested and may provide nutritious foods, such as buds, berries, seeds, etc., which can be eaten.

The following diagram will provide a good general pattern for skinning most animals. When the animal is too big to elevate, skin off one side to the centre of the back, then spread that skin out on the ground to protect the meat while you roll the animal over and skin the other side. All internal organs of game should be removed immediately to prevent bloating. Big game is usually bled out by the bullet which kills it; however, it is advisable to cut the jugular vein right after killing to assure thorough bleeding, hence better tasting and better keeping meat. The removal of internal organs from small game and birds may be left until return to camp.

Big game is more easily utilized when it has been butchered into manageable chunks as shown here.

Heart, liver, and kidneys of all game can be used (except as indicated above) and the eyes, brains, tongues, stomach lining, and even the stomach content of hooved animals can be consumed for roughage and vitamin content. Marrow of bones is also good. Be careful not to break the gall sack when removing the liver. Incidently, there is no gall sack in deer or other antlered game. In hooved animals all parts can be eaten. The same rule applies generally to small game.

BUTCHERING

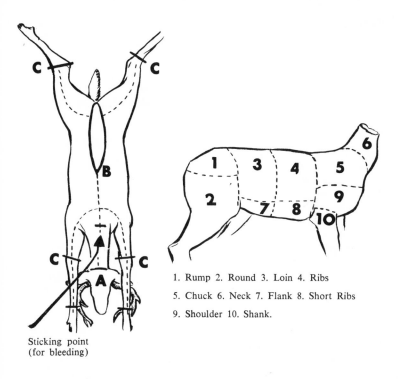

1. Rump 2. Round 3. Loin 4. Ribs
5. Chuck 6. Neck 7. Flank 8. Short Ribs
9. Shoulder 10. Shank.

Sticking point
(for bleeding)

A   Remove the head
B   Extend the cavity cut to A
C   Cut the hide the shortest distance from the cavity cut to C.
     Cut off the legs at C.

COOKING OF MEAT AND FISH

Boiling

    This is the best method of preparing meat for human consumption. It is easy, it requires less fuel than other methods, and, if you drink the resultant broth as well, you get the full food value. A small quantity will feed a number of people and there is no waste. In order to assure all meat is properly done, have the chunks of equal size.

127

A simple method of suspending the pot over the fire.

BOILING

Frying and Boiling

These can be done if the utensils are available and if there is sufficient food. A certain amount of the food value is wasted, and above the tree-line, where you may have only a limited quantity of fuel, you will waste fuel.

Barbecueing or Roasting

This is an easy method and often produces the tastiest results though it causes the most waste. Clean the fish or small animal and spike it on the end of a green stick elevated beside a hot fire, which produces as little smoke and flame as possible. If necessary turn the meat occasionally to assure it is thoroughly cooked. A great quantity of nutritious juices is lost by this method and there is considerable shrinkage. However this can be partially counteracted by either placing the meat very close to the fire at first to form a hard crust on the outside which will contain the juices, or having the meat suspended at one end of the fire with a shallow plate underneath to catch the drippings.

Broiling and Barbecueing or Roasting

Meat should be held to the side of hot coals not over them. Avoid smoke and flame. Use a receptacle to catch drippings.

Plank fish or meat on a split log with pegs.

Use a weight on the butt of the pole if necessary. The pole can be rotated to baste all sides of the meat.

Cooking by the Lone Survivor

For the lone survivor, who may find himself without cooking utensils, baking, steaming, and barbecueing are good methods to use.

To bake, hollow out a shallow pit and line it with rocks. Place over them a good bed of coals and on it place the food wrapped in sticky clay or mud. Meat, fish, and tubers can all be cooked by this method; the first should be in small pieces, e.g., a rabbit's leg. Over the food place more hot coals and cover the whole with a few inches of earth. Leave for an hour or so until cooked. The pit does not have to be lined with rocks, but foods cook faster and more thoroughly when they are used.

To steam, use the same rock lined pit but after burning the fire to achieve the bed of coals, scrape the coals out and replace them with wet or green grass. The food is wrapped as before (tin foil from rations is good—even dampened parachute material) and covered with a second layer of grass, then earth. Punch a hole down to the food level and pour in a small quantity of water. Then block the hole and leave for an hour or so to let the steam from the water on the hot rocks cook the food.

It is inadvisable for the survivor to eat meats and fish raw unless there is a complete lack of heat. Fish and many animals may be diseased or hosts to tapeworms, flukes, etc., which would be harmful to humans, but thorough cooking, e.g., boiling for 20 minutes, will kill almost any disease germ and all parasites.

A Simple Method of Baking Food.

PRESERVING OF MEATS AND FISH

To have a supply of food in excess of daily consumption is the objective of the survivor and if achieved, he must take steps to maintain the supply by avoiding spoilage and theft by small animals.

Freezing

In the winter this is no great problem; the food is frozen solid and stored in a place not accessible to animals. One thing to remember is that meat will spoil if thawed and re-frozen, particularly if this happens a number of times. Before freezing cut it into pieces of a size that can be used at one time and keep it frozen until ready to use.

Cooling

In the summer, small quantities which are to be kept for only a day or so, should remain as cool as possible. If a metal container with a lid is available, set it in water or bury it in damp earth, preferably in a shaded location. One method of cooling which has been successful is digging a hole in a river bank, lake shore, or hill side and blocking the entrance with a large piece of sod. Added cooling can be achieved by replacing the sod blocked door with a curtain of the heaviest possible material. This is saturated with water each morning and the evaporation process during the day will cool the chamber behind. The metal, or even wooden, container is to keep rodents from the food—the container should be ventilated. Remember that if it is excessively damp, meat will soon mould. Do not throw mouldy meat away; cut or scrape off the mould and cook as usual. In arctic and tundra areas dig to the perma-frost within a foot or two; no additional cooling is necessary.

Curing

The out-of-doors itself, sun, wind, etc, can be used to preserve. Larger pieces of meat can be suspended in trees above the fly line (the line above which insects are usually not found due to air turbulence) and the outer layer will dry into a hard crust which seals and protects the inner meat. In using this method be sure that separate pieces of meat are not touching each other as rotting will commence any place where the outer surface is not completely exposed. Fish and meat can be filleted and spread out on willow racks to be cured by the sun and wind. This is called "jerking" and is effective only in bright sunny weather. Meat can be best jerked by cutting it into strips about five inches by two inches by a quarter inch (or thinner).

Preserving Meat or Fish by Smoking

In warm or damp weather when meat and fish deteriorate rapidly it may be advisable to preserve the meat by smoke-curing. Smoking not only preserves the meat but also deters flies and like "jerking" it dehydrates and reduces weight.

(a) Lay strips of lean meat, one-quarter inch thick, on a green-wood grate three to four and a half feet above a slow-burning fire.

(b) Willow, alder, poplar, birch, and dwarf birch are suitable smoking woods, Resinous woods, such as spruce or pine, should not be used as they will blacken the meat and give it a disagreeable flavour.

(c) A tepee can be used as a smoke house to obtain a concentration of smoke.

(d) Avoid excessive heat and smoke. Do not let the heat cook the meat or draw out the juices. A sod-bank tunnel is a means of isolating the fire to provide a cooler supply of smoke.

(e) Continue smoking until the meat is brittle. It can then be eaten raw or cooked as desired, but avoid eating raw, smoked fresh water fish as they may contain parasites.

Tunnel covered completely
by bush or sod.

A Method of Smoking Meat or Fish

A Food Cache

A semi-isolated tree is less attractive to small climbers. Suspend the meat above the fly line and out of the reach of leaping animals. A piece of parachute material will protect the meat from the elements but leave it loose enough to allow free air circulation.

Caches

Surplus food and supplies should be cached. There are numerous methods of doing this. The best is to suspend the meat by rope, away from trees or uprights. The main threat to your cache is animals, from the bear to the mouse. The cache should be high enough to prevent attack from the ground, ten to fifteen feet, and far enough out from the uprights that climbing and springing animals will have difficulty reaching it. Squirrels and Canada Jays are the nuisances. Food can be covered to ward off meat-hungry birds, but from the preservation point of view it is advisable to have the cover fit loosely so that air can circulate around it. To do this have the cover also suspended by the rope and hanging around the meat. Have drying racks fairly high and if possible wrap the uprights with metal to stop climbers. Avoid overhanging branches.

132

APPENDIX A

Cat-tail
(Typha Latifolia)

Grows in marshy or wet ground. The flowering head is edible when young and green. Boil like asparagus.

The white succulent inner portion of the lower 12 to 15 inches of stem is widely used as food. Boil or eat raw.

Roots may be baked, boiled, or roasted. If woody, chew and swallow the starchy material. Spit out the residue.

Nutgrass
(Apios Apios or Apios Tuberosa)

Has a three-angled stem and grows in low ground near water.

Peel the root and eat raw or boiled. (Better boiled.)

The Ground Nut (Apois Americana) may be used in a similar manner.

Lichens

There are many varieties of lichens which can be eaten. Some can be nibbled raw but they are generally acidic and should be soaked in water for several hours then removed, dried, and crumbled, before boiling to a gelatinous consistency. May be used effectively in thickening soups, stews, etc., or as a broth.

Reindeer-Moss
(Cladonia-Rangiferina)

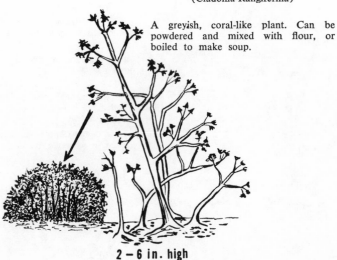

A greyish, coral-like plant. Can be powdered and mixed with flour, or boiled to make soup.

2 – 6 in. high

134

Dandelion
(Taraxacum Officinale)

The leaves are an excellent green. The
dried, ground-up roots make a substitute
for chicory which is a substitute for
coffee.

135

Bracken
(Pteridophytes)

Rootstalks are nutritious but quite woody. Roast or boil.

Fiddleheads or young curled up fern fronds make a delectable green when boiled.

The epithelium or tender growing portion at the base of the stem is good either raw or boiled.

Cow Parsnip
(Heracleam Lanatum)

Young leaves and flower stalks make a
sweet green. Eat raw or boil.

Liquorice Root
(Hedysarum Alpinum)

A vetch-like plant found in the northern
forests and on the tundra. The flowers
are pink-purplish and look somewhat
like pea blossoms. The roots are quite
substantial and can be eaten raw or
boiled.

137

Woolly Lousewort
(Pedicularis Lanata)

The roots and young flowering stems may be eaten raw or boiled. A common perennial of the arctic tundra, up to eight inches in height.

Lamb's Quarters or Pigweed
(Chenopodium Album)

Common throughout North America. The young leaves of this plant make an excellent green. Boil like spinach.

Stinging Nettle
(Urtica Dioica)

The leaves of the young plant make an excellent green. The bristled leaves and stems of the mature nettle produce a rash upon contact with the skin. Crushed dock leaves make an effective remedy for nettle stings.

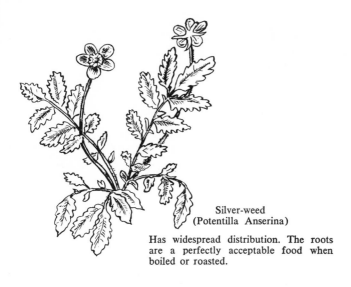

Silver-weed
(Potentilla Anserina)

Has widespread distribution. The roots
are a perfectly acceptable food when
boiled or roasted.

Lady's Slipper
(Cypripedium Acaule)

The roots may be boiled or eaten raw.

Tiger-lily or Turk's Cap Lily
(Lilium Superbum)

Has a brown spotted, orange flower. After peeling, the roots may be boiled or eaten raw.

Pond Lily
(Nuphar Species)

Widely distributed, the roots may be eaten if peeled and boiled. The seed pods are best when newly formed. Boil in two changes of water.

140

Labrador Tea
(Ledum Groenlandicum)

Widely distributed. Leaves make an
aromatic beverage somewhat like Chinese tea. Dry the leaves over fire in a
pan until they become crumbly. The
infusion is prepared by pouring boiling
water over the leaves. The resultant brew
is high in vitamin "C".

CARE OF
EQUIPMENT

Chapter 10

CARE AND USE OF EQUIPMENT AND CLOTHING

In the survivor's battle of man against nature, the odds greatly favor the man who is able to utilize his available equipment to the full and knows how to care for it.

It has been found that some persons have failed to survive, even under reasonably good conditions, not from lack of equipment but from failure to care for it and use it to the best advantage. Here are some suggestions for the proper care and use of the various pieces of equipment found in your survival kits, together with some suggestions for the fabrication of further survival aids.

Axe

This is one of the most important pieces of survival equipment, and also one of the most abused. Properly used it can simplify your survival problem, but misused, it can become a means of crippling yourself to such an extent that survival becomes impossible.

If your axe does not have a sheath, make one from any suitable material available, and keep the axe in its sheath until it is required for use. Before using, make the following checks.

(a) Check the head for tightness of the handle. If it is loose either drive the wedge further home or make a new wedge using hardwood. Soaking the head is another method but it is not recommended for winter time, as ice may form on the handle and inside the head, allowing the head to slide off and cause possible injury. To drive the handle further into the head, strike the end of the handle not the head of the axe.

(b) Check for sharpness. A dull axe can be dangerous for two reasons. First it will not bite properly and will tend to glance off the wood being cut. Secondly, when blunt it is necessary to use more force, which usually means a sacrifice of control.

(c) Check that the handle is not cracked or split. A serious cut or sliver might be received.

When carrying an axe, be sure that the sharp edge is held away from the body. In the event of a fall, there will then be less chance of injury.

When felling a tree, these procedures should be followed.

(a) Before beginning, clear the tree of lower limbs, and remove the underbrush from around the bottom of the tree. This is to ensure that the axe is not deflected during the swing.

(b) Check your distance from the tree to avoid underreaching or overreaching. Overreaching can result in breaking the axe handle: underreaching in a cut foot.

(c) Take up a comfortable stance, making sure that both feet are firmly set.

(d) The first cut should be made on the side of the tree facing the direction of the desired fall, often decided by the "lean" of the tree. This cut should be not more than half-way through the tree. The back cut should be commenced slightly above and opposite the first cut.

(e) It is safest to cut the tree off not over a foot above the ground. Always keep the axe handle low, i.e., parallel to the ground where the blade strikes the cut. When using short handled axes or hand axes bend fully at the hips or kneel on one knee.

When splitting wood, do not lay the piece to be split on the ground, but support it as illustrated. This not only prevents the axe from chopping into the ground and becoming blunted, but may also prevent injury to the legs or feet.

When finished with the axe, clean the head carefully, replace the sheath, and store in an upright position. It is permissible to store by sticking it in a dry stump, but green wood should never be used for this purpose.

Always stick your axe
in a log or stump

Knife

As with the axe, the knife should be kept sharp and carried in a stout sheath. Return it to the sheath immediately after use. Always position the sheath on your belt towards the back of the hip, since with the knife in a forward position it is possible that a fall could drive the knife into the groin.

Guard against loss by attaching a cord from the handle of the knife to your belt or belt loop. Never throw your knife. It is ineffective when so misused and it will probably be damaged or lost.

Firearms

To the survivor who has had experience in the handling of firearms and has acquired a degree of proficiency in their use, a rifle or shotgun can be an invaluable asset. Practice firing on a range is the best method of getting acquainted with the weapons used in the service, and facilities exist at most units for such practice. It is recommended that all aircrew take advantage of these facilities and become as proficient as possible in the handling and firing of firearms.

Rules for the proper care of your weapons are as follows.

(a) In cold weather, store your firearms in a sheltered cold spot. Avoid moving between the warm shelter and cold outdoors as eventually, because of the condensation of moisture on the metal parts, the protective blueing will break down and allow the metal to rust. Also remove grease and oil from the weapon and replace them with non-freezing oil or graphite. If neither is available, the moving parts can be rubbed with a pencil or the gun can be used without lubrication.

(b) Keep the barrel clean at all times. A plugged barrel may cause a firearm to explode, with serious injury to the user.

(c) Always prove your weapon when storing it or picking it up. "Empty" guns have caused many fatalities.

(d) Store guns and ammunition in a safe dry place.

Snow Saw-Knife

In arctic survival, the snow saw-knife is one of the most useful tools in your possession. Guard against loss by sticking it upright in the snow when not in use. At night take it into the shelter with you, because it may be necessary to cut your way out in the morning. Avoid chopping ice or frozen meat with it; under extremely cold conditions this can chip or shatter the blade.

Ice Chisel

As with all edged tools, it should be kept sharp. The sectional handle should be checked for rigidity before use, and the joints shimmed where necessary. If a cord loop is not supplied, make one and attach it to the end of the handle, looping it over your wrist when using the chisel. This will guard against loss when the chisel breaks through the ice.

Sleeping Bag

In summer, keep it dry, air it when weather conditions permit, and shake it daily. Roll up lightly when not in use.

In winter, keep it free of snow. Open it completely every morning and gently beat off any frost which may have formed during the night. Roll the bag up lightly and cover it to protect it from the snow when not in use. Air your sleeping bag as often as weather will permit, shaking it gently to restore resiliency to the feathers. If using wood fires for heat, guard against spark damage. If a hole should occur in your bag repair it immediately. Considerable loss of insulation will result if a hole is not repaired when first noticed.

Clothing

It is even more important to keep your clothing clean and in good repair while on survival than it is during your everyday life in the city.

Good hygiene is of course essential and the clothes on your back may be the only ones you have till you are picked up.

Use your clothing wisely, making every effort to keep it clean and dry at all times. If your clothes become wet, dry them as soon as possible. Socks and mitts particularly should be kept dry. These will usually get damp during a day's wearing. Unless too damp they can be dried quite effectively by placing them in your sleeping bag before retiring and leaving them there for the night. If a hole is worn in a sock, turn the sock over to prevent a blister on the heel.

In winter, dress lightly when exerting yourself, and have extra clothing handy to put on when sitting around idle.

When working in a parka, it is wise to drop the hood and allow the warm air around your body to escape. The hood can be raised again when work is completed.

In the Arctic, damp clothing can be left to freeze and the moisture beaten out of it when frozen.

In the bush, clothing may be dried by the fire. Take the following precautions.

(a) Never place clothing nearer to the fire than you can comfortably hold your hand.

(b) Never leave clothing by an untended fire.

(c) When drying leather foot-wear, turn it and work the leather periodically to keep it pliable. When almost completely dry, apply a good coating of dubbin or fat, working the grease well into the seams and pores of the leather. Do not heat leather.

Miscellaneous Equipment

Your kit will contain many small items which can easily become lost if not looked after. The following rules apply to such pieces of gear which are not usually carried on the person but are used by everyone in the party.

(a) Have a designated place for the equipment, and return it after use. Have this location well marked, and make everyone in the party aware of its existence.

(b) Never lay equipment down on snow, spruce boughs, or ground. Put it in your pocket or hang it in a conspicuous place.

(c) Locate your equipment in an accessible place, so that you can reach such items as your signal flares, at a moment's notice.

(d) Small items, such as compass, match container, etc., should be tied to the person while travelling to avoid loss.

Other General Rules

Do not cut rope or twine unless absolutely necessary, as you may need it later in its original length.

Make sure your cooking is done on level solid ground to guard against tipping.

Fill your Primus stove, lantern, etc., away from your shelter, and over some utensil that will catch spills, thus reducing waste and eliminating the fire hazard.

Make a habit of tying knots which can easily be undone, such as the bowline, clove hitch, etc., particularly in cold weather.

Do not throw away scraps of cloth, bits of twine, metal, and so on. You may find a use for them later.

Keep your cooking and eating utensils clean. Any abrasive material, such as sand or wood ash or a combination of both, makes a good substitute for soap.

During the arctic spring (April to June) and in winter bush snow conditions, sun-glasses, improvised or otherwise, should be used continuously. As long as the sun is up, especially on slightly overcast days there is a danger of snow blindness. If your glasses become steamed up while working, do not discard them but try to provide more ventilation. Snow blindness can be serious.

Improvised Equipment

There will be a number of tools or appliances which would be most useful, but which are not contained in your survival kit. With the use of salvaged material such as metal wire from the aircraft, fabric, cord, and webbing from the parachute and harness, and the natural materials around you, you are limited only by your ability and ingenuity in the production of gadgets to make yourself more comfortable.

Here are a few ideas which have been developed in the past.

(a) needles from bone or metal parts of the aircraft;

(b) fish lures from various combinations of wood, metal, and brightly coloured cloth;

(c) snow knives from wood, metal, or bone;

(d) water bottles from bark, the internal organs and skins of animals, and waterproof materials from the aircraft;

(e) good whisk brooms from wings of birds;

(f) eating utensils from bone, wood, or metal; and

(g) eye snow shields from wood or from cloth.

The bow drill principle can be used for drilling holes in objects.

The Parachute

The parachute is probably the most useful single item available to the survivor, if he is ingenious enough to utilize it fully.

The canopy can provide:

(a) shelters;

(b) signal strips;

(c) clothing;

(d) sleeping robes;

(e) sails;

(f) wrappers for meat and fish; and

(g) bandages.

The shroud lines have a woven case and seven twisted threads, each thread consisting of three smaller threads. The complete line will lift about 500 pounds. They can be used for:

(a) snares to catch anything from a "moose to a mouse;

(b) fish lines—one thread, waxed;

(c) fish nets—woven from threads;

(d) ropes, lines, sewing thread and sutures;

(e) lifelines and lashings; and

(f) snow-shoe webbing.

The pack can provide:

(a) knapsack;

(b) foot-wear, mittens, and headgear; and

(c) axe and knife holsters.

Miscellaneous

Item	
(a) Wire frame	Fish spear
(b) Release Pins	Fish hooks
(c) Harness webbing	Belts, pack straps, and tump-lines
(d) Steel plates (chest packs)	Fair quality knives
(e) Bungee cords or pack bands	Catapults

TRAVEL

CHAPTER 11

TRAVEL

A survey of survival incidents both in the Canadian Forces and USAF has indicated that travel is not to be recommended except under conditions when the aircraft has been forced down in an area where survival might prove difficult or dangerous. Under these circumstances, travel should be only as far as is necessary to find a good safe dry location for your camp.

Each survival incident, however, must be considered with regard to its own specific problems, and the decision as to whether or not to travel must be made by you, the survivor, and made quickly. If you do decide to travel, you must travel while you still have strength.

There are five basic requirements for travel. If any one of these cannot be fulfilled to your specific situation, then don't travel.

(a) Know where you are and where you are going. If you do not know where you have landed, you can rarely plan a route to safety. Stay put!

(b) Have a means of setting and maintaining direction. If you have a hand compass and know how to use it, you should be able to maintain a planned course. If you have not, then you will have to use the Big Dipper and pole-star, or the watch-and-sun method, which will be described later. If you have no sure means of determining and maintaining a heading—sit tight!

(c) Most people are inclined to over-estimate their physical capabilities. Even if you are athletically inclined, able to walk five or six miles round a golf course in balmy summer weather, it is no indication of how far you are likely to travel through boggy country or hip deep snow. Be very very careful when trying to estimate your physical stamina, and if in doubt—don't start out!

(d) Clothes make the man. This is particularly true in survival when the proper clothing can mean the difference between life and death. Proper clothing is important for all seasons of the year, as it affords protection not only against the elements but also against the almost inconceivable torture from bites by the hordes of insects

155

that abound in Canada's summer northland. Adequate foot-wear is perhaps the most important item of clothing. Wet socks can cause grave discomfort and may completely incapacitate a man. Wind-proof clothing is a necessity in cold weather and should be worn over an insulating type of underclothing such as woollen under-wear. Unless your clothing is sufficient to protect you from any conditions which you may encounter—sit and wait!

(e) Food, fuel, shelter and signals, must be considered in relation to the type of country and the season. The emergency rations normally carried in aircraft will be of little help as they are not designed for active survival. They provide much less than the caloric intake required for travel and must be supplemented. Fuel is no problem in bush country, but travel on the tundra, especially in winter, will mean transporting sufficient fuel. A small mis-calculation could be fatal. It is advisable to carry sufficient materials to construct a basic shelter. A piece of parachute cloth or tarpaulin is all that is required. A sleeping bag should be carried during all seasons. Signalling aids are a necessity for the survivor and constitute a definite requirement while travelling. The heliograph mirror and pyrotechnics should be carried in your pockets or on the top of your pack, where they can be put to use at a moment's notice.

The following equipment is suggested for most situations; sleeping bag, fabric for shelter, waterproof match container (full), food, candles, cooking utensils, axe, knife, gun and ammunition, fishing gear, maps, compass, extra clothing, first aid kit, sewing kit, sun-glasses, signal mirror, and pyrotechnics. These are all small items, but considering them together in relation to (c), it is enough to make you pause and reconsider. Remember, if it looks like a rough go you will be far better off to remain where you are.

BUSH TRAVEL

Summer

Bush travel in summer is relatively easy, if the following rules are followed.

Before any bush trip, climb a high hill or large tree to orient yourself with the surrounding area and possibly discover human habitation.

Game trails provide an easy path through bush country. The main game trails follow the ridges and river flats and are connected by a network of trails. The danger in following these trails lies in the fact that, unless you keep a careful check on direction, you may wander off your heading.

Streams may be followed to larger rivers or lakes, along the shores of which you are mostly likely to find habitation. Generally, it is better to follow the drainage pattern than to cross it.

Rivers may be followed along the bank, but the winding nature of rivers usually means travelling about four times as far to get from A to B as opposed to ridge travel. Unless the water-ways in the survival area are well known to the survivors, raft building is not recommended.

Ridges offer drier, more insect-free, travel than bottom land. There will usually be less underbrush and as a result it will be easier to see and be seen.

Larger river crossing should be attempted only when absolutely necessary. If the water is deep remove all clothing, placing it in a bundle, and replace your boots without socks. Boots give better footing on the river bottom and prevent injury to the feet during crossing. If forced to swim in fast flowing rivers, start up-stream from your proposed landing place and let the current drift you down to it. When fording a fast shallow stream use a pole to help maintain footing, by placing the butt-end down on the up-stream side.

Decide whether to cross or go around each lake. If it is decided to cross, use a raft or floatation gear to assist. Swimming cold waters can be risky. Play it safe.

Deadfall and swamps should be avoided. Deadfall can be dangerous, because of the ever present danger of slipping and injury. Swamps can also be dangerous, but their main problem is the steady sapping of strength because of difficult walking conditions. Go around them.

Mountain areas have their own particular problems. Watch for overhead threats, shale slides, etc. When crossing shale slopes, it is advisable to rope the party together, and send one man at a time across the slope, using the remainder of the party as an anchor against a possible slide. In early spring, cross mountain streams in early morning to avoid the greatest volume of water, which occurs when the sun starts melting the snow. When crossing snow slopes in summer, it is less dangerous to cross them early in the morning when they will have a hard crust.

Winter

Game trails, especially if heavily used, will save walking through deep snow, but you must avoid being led off your general heading.

Streams and rivers will provide your best method of travel, being the highways of the Canadian north. There are however, dangers in winter river travel which must be carefully watched for and avoided. In certain places along the river, weak ice will be found, and it is best to know in advance where to look for it.

(a) Stay away from rocks and other protrusions, since ice formation in these localities will have been retarded by eddies.

(b) Walk on the inside of curves, since on the outside of curves the river current has an eroding effect on the under side of the ice surface.

(c) Take to the bank or walk on the opposite side of the river at the junction of two rivers, because the currents from both rivers hold up the formation of the ice through turbulence.

(d) Stay on clear ice when possible since a deep layer of snow will insulate and retard freezing, and erosion by the river may leave only a snow bridge.

(e) Carry a pole for testing ice and for use in supporting your weight if you break through.

(f) Be prepared to get rid of your pack if you should fall through the ice.

(g) Before beginning any trip on ice be certain that a good waterproof fire starting kit is immediately available and will not be lost.

(h) You may encounter overflow under the snow. Wet feet will freeze rapidly.

Ridges may give easier walking conditions as they do not usually have the same amount of snow as the valleys.

Mountain areas, in winter, can be particularly treacherous, with the possibility of snow slides, uncertain footing and sudden storms. Snow slides will occur from natural causes, but care should be taken to avoid causing them through carelessness.

Deadfall is even more dangerous in winter than in summer since a lot of it will be covered by snow, making walking conditions extremely treacherous.

BARREN LAND TRAVEL

Snow-shoes and skis are not essential on hard snow. On the Arctic Islands and barrens east of the 142nd meridian, walking conditions are normally good in winter. In some localities frequent gales are encountered. There is no shelter except that provided by scattered high banks and willow thickets around lakes and along stream beds. Game is very scarce and fires cannot be maintained for long on the fuel generally to be found in the dead of winter. The survivor cannot afford to follow the streams which, because of their winding nature, double and quadruple the distance to be covered. The compass is not reliable and landmarks are few and far between. One man will have difficulty steering a straight course by himself. Two can do a little better but three are required to navigate when visibility is low. It is recommended that any extended travel over barren land or sea ice be done by a party of at least three for this reason.

The spring break-up, summer, and the fall freeze present far greater travel difficulties than does the winter season. Equipment must be racked on the back. The masses of soggy vegetation on the tundra cause the traveller to slip and slide. Lake systems must be either crossed or circumnavigated. Care must be taken in crossing sand-bars and mud flats at the mouths and junctions of rivers, and lake and lagoon outlets. Quicksands or bottomless muck may trap you. If a life raft is available, it is preferable to float down a river rather than attempt to travel across country. The months of July and August are about the best summer months for cross country travel. Because of the prevalence of fish in all streams or lakes, a fish net is one of the best pieces of equipment the traveller can carry. A rifle may provide game for a number of meals.

SEA ICE TRAVEL

Food in the form of seal, fox, and polar bear is more readily obtained on winter sea ice than on barren land. Unless serious injury prevents travel, do not split up the party as there is generally nothing to be gained by anyone who remains behind. All should travel at once.

The problems of navigation are identical with those on the barren lands with one very great exception. The polar ice pack is in constant motion. This is caused by current and wind. Therefore, determination of direction may be particularly difficult. Also one rarely travels in a straight line, but follows the smooth going and avoids the rough ice. Landmarks in the form of high pressure ridges and hummocks are usable only over short distances, since it may be that they are located on other floes which are changing position. Add to this the fact that the magnetic compass is very unreliable in high latitudes and the necessity for constant directional checks on the sun and stars becomes obvious.

The ice in the very high latitudes is comparatively solid in winter. As the sun returns the ice recedes and there is open water along the entire arctic coast. Along the north coast, ice lies off shores, and with strong north or west winds floes are often driven ashore. Riding one of these floes is definitely a last resort procedure, since there is no guarantee that the wind will continue until the floe grounds. Ice floes in the fall are less dangerous as they will usually not travel too far before they freeze in again.

The summer ice is covered with lakes and water soaked snow, which gradually drain off as the ice develops holes and cracks. There is practically no dry surface anywhere. Fogs abound and misting rain is frequent. All that has been said about winter travel applies to summer travel. Survivors should leave the ice and get to land if this is possible. Travel should otherwise be restricted to a minimum since it will avail little and it is dangerous and exhausting.

Cracks in stationary ice, e.g., on sounds or bays, do not pose any great problem during the winter, and in the spring and summer they are readily seen and have to be circumnavigated via their narrow end. Cracks in moving ice can be opened and closed quite suddenly by wind and tide pressures and one should be on the alert for them at all times, using both eyes and ears.

All icebergs frozen in the ice are likely to have open water in their vicinity. This is because of the force exerted by the current on the greater mass of the berg below the surface. Icebergs driven by the currents have been known to crash through ice several feet in thickness. Towering icebergs are always a danger in open water. The area below the surface melts faster than that in the air. When the berg's equilibrium is upset, it topples over, and the adjoining area is no place for man or beast. The resulting tidal waves throw the surrounding small ice pieces in all directions. Therefore, stay away from pinnacled bergs. Seek out low, flat topped bergs for shelter at sea.

TRAVEL HINTS—SUMMARY

General

Take it easy. Conserve energy. If you are tired, stop and make camp.

Carry adequate but only necessary equipment. Don't overload. Keep your equipment in good condition; guard against losses; and protect food from prowling animals.

Be prepared to signal passing planes.

Don't travel alone if it can be avoided. Mark the trail and leave messages wherever possible.

To follow a straight line choose two easily visible points ahead in line along the route. Then travel keeping the two points in line. Looking back occasionally will also help to keep you in line with your departure point.

Plot your course on a map.

Improvise travel aids such as snow-shoes, sleds, rafts, and packs.

Keep a log-book of your travels.

Take care of your feet.

In Summer

Dense vegetation, rough terrain, insects, soft ground, swamps, lakes, and large rivers are obstacles to foot travel.

Cross glacier-fed streams in early morning to avoid the maximum volume.

Travel on ridges and game trails is the easiest method—maintain constant direction checks.

In Winter

Soft deep snow, dangerous river ice, severe weather and a scarcity of natural food are major obstacles in winter travel.

Don't travel in a blizzard or during extremely cold weather. Hole up and save your strength.

When travelling on frozen rivers be wary of thin ice, overflows, heavy snow, and air pockets. Use a pole or ice chisel for testing ice. Rope together when forced to cross dangerous ice.

If you do break through ice get into shelter and start a fire.

Guard against frost-bite.

In Mountains

In this region, routes should be chosen to lead you:

(a) out of a dangerous location to a more sheltered area;
(b) to the seacoast;
(c) to a major river; or
(d) to some known point of habitation.

Travel on a trail, down a river, or along a seacoast will usually lead to a cache, a cabin, or a settlement.

The larger rivers in the interior of Alaska and Canada are main lines of summer and winter travel.

Use the topography to the best advantage. Travel with drainage lines not across them, particularly in summer.

Avoid climbing if possible.

Messages

These should be left at every stop, with the initial message being left at the crash scene. A message should also be left at any point at which a change in plans is put into effect. The message should contain the following information:

(a) date of leaving the crash scene;

(b) destination and route;

(c) estimated length of the journey;

(d) number in the party;

(e) physical condition of the party; and

(f) any other pertinent data regarding supplies, etc.

Make certain the message is left in a readily accessible place. Lacking a pen or pencil, messages may be written with charcoal.

Uses of Compass

The Silva Prospector is the compass packed in Canadian Forces survival kits at the present time. It may be used as a protractor or as a compass.

Using the Compass as a Protractor

Draw a straight line along your desired direction of travel indicating A as the present location and B as the intended destination. This line is your required track.

Place the compass along this track as shown in Figure 1.

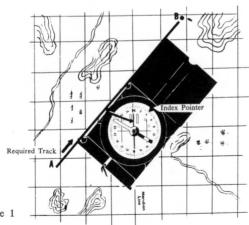

Figure 1

Rotate the compass housing until the compass meridian lines on the transparent compass face are parallel to the meridian lines of the map and north (N) points to true north on the map as in Figure 1.

The compass face is marked off around the perimeter in 2 degree intervals represented by a short line, a larger line every 10 degrees, and Arabic numbers every 20 degrees. The number 2 represents 020 degrees, and number 4 represents 040 degrees, number 26 represents 260 degrees, and so on with north (N) representing 360 degrees.

Now read off your required track opposite the index pointer. In Figure 1, your required track would be approximately 040 true.

Variation

You now have the required track true. In order to travel along this required track, you must allow for local magnetic variation. In other words, you must compensate for the angle between true north and magnetic north. Variation will be either easterly or westerly and is always indicated on topographic maps.

A good rule for applying variation is:

Variation east—magnetic least; and
Variation west—magnetic best.

EXAMPLE. Figure 1 indicates that your required track from A to B is 040 degrees true. Let us assume that the local variation is 20 degrees east. Therefore, according to our rule, we would subtract 20 degrees easterly variation from our required track true of 040 degrees. This gives us a magnetic heading of 020 degrees which is set on the compass opposite the index pointer.

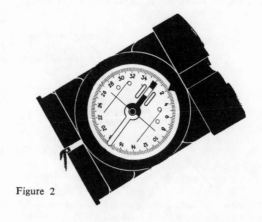

Figure 2

How to Use the Compass

With the magnetic heading established and set on the compass it is now ready for travel.

With the compass held in your hand turn yourself around until the "Red End" or north seeking pole is pointing to north (N) on the compass face and the magnetic needle is parallel to the two luminous lines.

Figure 3

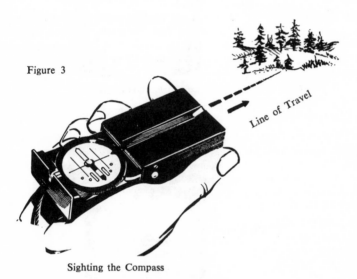

Sighting the Compass

Sighting the Compass

The compass is now pointing along the required track and a sighting line may be obtained as illustrated in Figure 3.

The magnetic needle is read between the two luminous compass orienting lines by its reflection in the sighting mirror. In using the sighting mirror, you can see that, when the needle is oriented between the two parallel lines, it appears to be closer to one line than it is to the other. This would give the impression that it is not exactly in the centre (Figure 4). However, this is easily explained. The mirror, slanted as it is at a 41 degree angle, influences the reflection according to the laws of parallax. In using the sighting mirror, therefore, parallel the needle with the orienting line which appears nearest to it, and accurate results will follow. Be sure to level the compass while using the sighting mirror.

Right

The magnetic needle is closer to one of the lines than it is to the other.

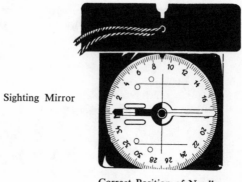

Sighting Mirror

Correct Position of Needle

Figure 4

Sighting Mirror

Wrong Position of Needle

Wrong

The magnetic needle appears to be centred between the two luminous lines, but is not parallel to them.

Choose a landmark to which the sighting line points (rock, tree, etc). Walk directly to that landmark. When you have arrived at your landmark, sight again, choose a new landmark or target, and travel to it as before. By moving from new landmark to new landmark, you will describe a straight path through the country-side to your destination.

Measurement of Distance

A simple means of determining distance would be an asset at times, when walking, e.g.:

(a) to survey the crash area and explore its potential;

(b) to make a dogleg detour in order to resume track on the opposite side of an obstacle; and

(c) to orient oneself on the ground to a 16 mile/1 inch map is not easy—relating actual distances on the ground to scaled distances on the map will simplify the task of interpreting the map.

One method of estimating distance is the tally and pace system. It is based on the 30 inch pace which is adopted for most military drill work. This is neither a long nor a short pace for most people. It is a pace which you probably use every day.

1 pace	=30 inches
1 double pace (i.e., each time the same foot touches the ground)	=60 inches=5 feet
66 double paces	=330 feet=1 tally (tie a knot in a string for each tally)
16 tallies	=5,280 feet=1 mile.

Map Reading

While it may not be possible for you to learn all the symbols shown on various maps, it is as well to know the ones which indicate difficult or impossible travel or aid locations. Generally speaking these are as follows:

(a) Swamps or Marshes. The dotted lines indicate that the exact shore line of the marsh or swamp is not known.

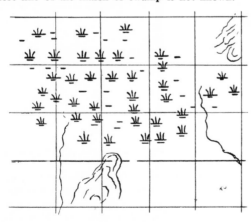

Swamp or Marsh

165

(b) Undulating Country. The height of the ground is indicated by a continuous line joining all points of equal height. The variation in height will differ depending on the scale of the map and the terrain which it covers.

This shows that a steep slope is represented by contour lines close together while a shallow slope has contour lines far apart.

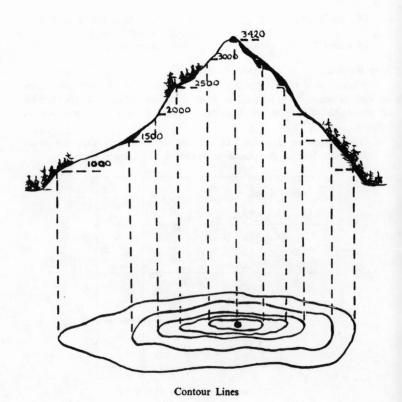

Contour Lines

166

(c) Rapids. These are shown as a series of light lines drawn across the river covering the area in which the rapids occur. They are usually marked only on navigable rivers.

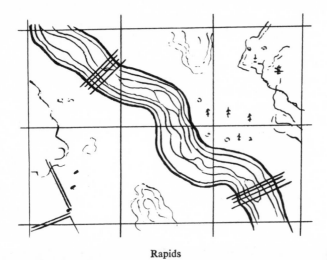

Rapids

(d) Falls. These are generally shown as a light double line drawn directly across a river, with the word "falls" written alongside, and a figure indicating the drop in feet.

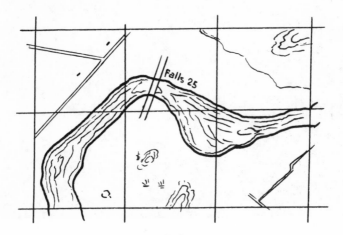

Falls

(e) Trails. These are usually shown as dotted lines, either single or double. A single line usually denotes a pack trail, while double lines usually indicate a trail used by wagons or tractors.

(f) Cabins. Ranger stations, etc., are marked as black squares with "Cabin", "Mission", or "Lookout Tower" written alongside. Trading posts are shown as black squares with TR written alongside.

It is best to remember that the shortest distance between two points is not necessarily the quickest route. Pick your route carefully to give you easy walking conditions, even if it does add a few miles to the trip. It will pay off in the long run.

Finding Direction Without a Compass

Three methods of finding North are discussed here.

(a) The first, by using the pole-star, is the easiest. Having found the pole-star, simply face it and you are facing North. To find the pole-star, the Big Dipper or Plough is used.

The Big Dipper and Pole-Star

168

(b) The second method, using the sun and your watch, is a little more complicated, but reasonably accurate. First, by orienting your watch, point the hour hand directly at the sun. Then by bisecting the angle between the hour hand and twelve o'clock you have an imaginary line running north and south. For example, at 8 am it would appear thus:

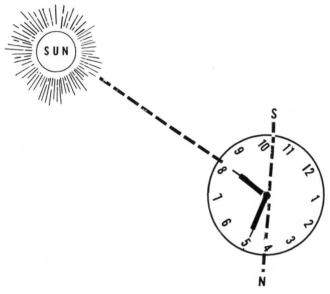

Using the Sun and a Watch to Determine a North-South Line

Remember, in the Arctic, when the sun is up all day, any confusion between 12 midnight and 12 noon could cause an 180 degree error in direction. In the example shown above, had the observation been at 8 pm rather than 8 am, the direction would be reversed. Make sure your watch is on local or standard time.

(c) The third method of finding north is to place a long stick in the ground, and as the sun progresses place shorter twigs in the ground at the end of the shadows. The shortest shadow will indicate north, or a line drawn from one short twig to another will indicate the east-west line.

Blazing

Blazing serves more than one purpose on a survival trek. It will not only be a guide to a ground search party, but will also help the survivor to find his way back to the crash scene should he change his mind about travelling.

In the bush, blazes should be placed on both sides of trees.

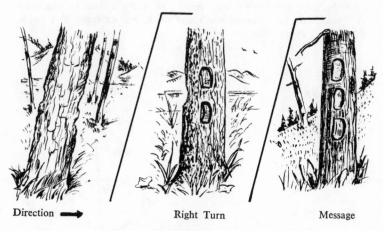

Direction ➡   Right Turn   Message

Tree Blazing

In short growth, saplings may be snapped.

170

In grassy clearings, where trees are not available, long grass may be tied together in bunches.

In the Arctic, or bush country in winter, where nothing else is available, snow blocks may be used to mark a trail.

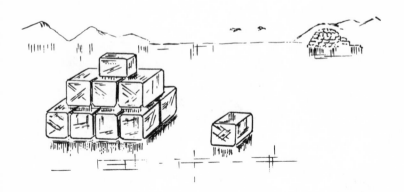

In summer use rocks or sod blocks.

SEA SURVIVAL

CHAPTER 12

SEA SURVIVAL

To have to survive a bail out or ditching at sea is probably the most formidable experience one can expect to be faced with. Man's natural environment is land and every action he must perform in a sea survival situation must be learned either through study or practice.

When one considers that approximately 71 per cent of the earth's surface is covered with salt water aircrew can expect to fly over salt water for a large percentage of their service career. In the event of an emergency, when flying over the sea, it will probably not be possible to reach shore prior to having to bail out or ditch the aircraft.

Survival at sea is undoubtedly the most severe survival situation that man can be exposed to. To survive for any reasonable length of time, even in tropical waters, one must have protection from exposure, water to drink, and protection from various dangers of the sea. In short, one must have survival equipment in the form of flotation equipment, a means of protecting himself from the elements and other danger, as well as drinking water, or a means of procuring it if survival is going to be successful. In addition, a survivor or survivors at sea must have artificial methods of attracting the attention of search aircraft or vessels, if rescue is expected. A life raft at sea is very difficult to spot from the air particularly if there are waves and/or if the area one may be down in has not been pinpointed. For aircrew the life preserver, life rafts, and ancillary equipment available provide these life support aids. However, having the equipment alone is not sufficient—one must know how to use the equipment properly, how to take care of it and how to get the most out of it if one is to survive until rescued.

Preparation for Sea Survival, as for any survival, must start long before the emergency arises. This includes being aware of the possibility of an emergency, knowing what survival equipment is available, its location in the aircraft, and above all, knowing your bail out procedures and/or ditching drill.

The Sea, like the Arctic and desert is unforgiving; any serious mistake will probably be your last.

Immediate Actions After Ditching

The life raft should be boarded directly from the aircraft, if possible. Step into the raft—do not jump in. If the raft inflates upside down one man should enter the sea and right it. If it is necessary for all survivors to get into the water before boarding the raft, one man should board the raft first, then assist any injured personnel aboard. Ditching suits should be worn by all, if available.

Roll should be called or a head count taken, before cutting loose from the aircraft to ensure all personnel are accounted for and to make certain all survival equipment is on board the raft.

The raft should now be cut adrift from the aircraft and paddled free before the fuselage sinks. If more than one life raft is used they should rendezvous and tie the rafts together with a piece of line approximately 25 feet long. This will prevent the rafts from rubbing together and will also prevent them from jerking with the wave action which could result in damage to the rafts. All equipment should now be lashed to the raft and one occupant of each raft should attach himself to the raft with a length of line. This is a precaution to prevent the raft from drifting out of reach in the event it overturns. Check the ballast pockets to ensure they fill with water and stream the sea anchor. This line should be adjusted so that the sea anchor will remain in the trough of a wave or swell when the raft is at the crest.

Administer first aid as required as soon as possible.

If weather is adverse, erect the canopy or if your raft has a self inflating canopy close the side curtains. Check the raft for damage, top up the buoyancy chambers if not firm enough. These should be firm but not drum tight.

Bale out the water, finishing off with the sponge. With patience it is possible to eliminate all water from the raft in this manner. If clothing is wet, it should be removed and wrung as dry as possible, then put back on prior to final sponging of the raft floor.

You should now prepare all of your signalling devices and have them available for immediate use. Use your emergency radio in accordance with instructions and at the prescribed times.

Activate the desalter kits and solar stills, if available, in accordance with instructions.

A definite plan of action should be taken. Normally, the aircraft captain takes charge but he may elect to delegate someone more experienced. Good leadership is of utmost importance. Duties should be allocated to all uninjured personnel.

Immediate Actions Upon Water Entry after Bail out

As you are descending in your parachute you should activate your life preserver and take the necessary action to deploy your seat pack, if the type of equipment you have dictates this procedure.

As you enter the water you should release yourself from the parachute by pressing the quick release box (after unlocking it) and clear the leg straps. In the case of parachutes employing the Capewell releases, activate the releases on water entry and remain in the harness.

If the canopy settles over you in the water—stay calm, float in your life preserver, and without kicking your feet pull the canopy off by following one shroud line to the edge of the canopy. Clear all shroud lines from your legs and other possible areas where they may be entangled and swim away from the canopy.

If the wind is blowing so strong as to keep the canopy inflated, it will undoubtedly pull you through the water if you have not either released your Capewell releases or activated the quick release box and cleared the leg straps. If this should happen, to prevent drowning, and if you are not already on your back, roll over, bend sharply at the waist and spread your legs. This will put you in a planing position to prevent you from porpoising through the water. At this time, take the necessary action to release yourself from the canopy.

As soon as you are free of the canopy, pull your life raft to you, if it was inflated in the air, and board it. If it was not inflated in the air, inflate it at this time. Do not hold on to the CO_2 bottle as you can receive a frost bite from it as the bottle inflates the raft.

If your parachute harness is equipped with Capewell releases, ensure the covers are closed. Board the raft from the foot or narrow end by grasping the handles on either side and pulling it down and under you. Then progressively pull and squirm the rest of the way into the raft taking care not to puncture or tear it. Roll over in the raft and take up a sitting position.

Ensure the ballast bags are filled with water and stream the sea anchor (it is normally stowed in the forward ballast bag). If necessary adjust the sea anchor line so that it remains in the trough of the wave when the raft is at the crest.

Bale out the raft, wring as much water out of your clothing as possible, bring your equipment pack aboard, and finish bailing using the sponge until the raft floor is virtually dry. If weather is inclement and you continue to ship water pull the spray shield over your head and close it completely.

If the raft is too soft, top it with air using the hand bellows. It should not be drum tight as it will ride too light in the water and be very susceptible to capsizing. It is better to have it soft enough to bend with the waves.

Keep the raft and all equipment tied to your person with a length of line to prevent loss in the event of capsizing or accidentally dropping equipment overboard.

Life Raft Environment

If the raft becomes damaged it should be patched immediately with the patches provided. Improvised patches can be effected by using adhesive tape from the medical kit or other adhesive tape that may be available from other parts of kits even though it has been previously used. Tape will stick best if the raft surface is dry.

Air expansion caused from direct sun on the raft or air contraction from cold air at night might make it necessary to bleed off or top up air to maintain the correct firmness of the raft.

Keep your mind occupied with the task at hand and relax. In a group, pull together as a team, ensure everyone has a job to do. This will help time to pass and will also help to minimize the possibility of sea sickness.

Medical Care and Health Protection

Treat any injuries as detailed in Chapter 4. Place any casualties on the floor of the raft and make them as comfortable as possible. Insulation will be required between the floor of the raft and the patient to help keep him as warm and dry as possible.

In addition to treatment of injuries, there are a number of factors that can affect your health and well being that are peculiar to a Sea Survival situation. These are chiefly caused by shortage of fresh water and exposure to the weather and salt water.

Exposure to Wind and Sun

a. do not expose yourself needlessly to the sun and wind. In hot climates it is better to keep a light layer of clothing on than to shed all clothing. If extremely hot, a cooling effect can be obtained by dipping clothing in the sea, wringing it out, and putting it back on. Use anti-sunburn cream on areas of skin that must be exposed;

b. the treatment for windburn or sunburn is to apply an antiseptic emulsion and cover.

Sore Eyes

a. wear sun glasses or eye shields as the reflection off the water will intensify the sun's rays causing sore eyes, very quickly. Remember that even on an overcast day this precaution should be taken; and

b. if eyes do become sore, do not rub them. Apply an antiseptic cream to the eyelids and bandage lightly.

Seasickness

a. keeping your mind occupied with various chores will help to prevent seasickness. Every effort should be made to remain relaxed.

b. if you become seasick do not eat or drink, lie still, relax and try to keep as warm as possible. If you have anti-seasick tablets use them.

Immersion Foot

a. this is caused by exposure of feet and legs to cold water for prolonged periods. It is recognized by a red coloring and pain. Following this, in extreme cases, the affected area will swell and blisters will appear interspersed with dark blotches on the skin;

b. prevention is possible by keeping the feet as warm and dry as possible. Keeping the raft floor dry will assist. Tight fitting boots should be removed; and

c. treatment consists of moving feet and toes to assist blood circulation. Do not massage them. Keep them as dry and warm as possible by wrapping in pieces of dry clothing or dry parachute cloth. Keep the feet raised clear of any water and keep the body warm.

Salt Water Sores

    a.   these are caused by prolonged exposure to salt water. Prevention lies in keeping all clothing as dry as possible; and

    b.   the sores should be cleaned and an antiseptic cream applied. If they are large they should be covered with a dressing. Do not squeeze the sores.

Parched Lips and Cracked Skin

Prevention and treatment are the same. Apply sun screen cream or vaseline and do not lick your lips. Cover to prevent further drying out by sun and wind, if possible.

Constipation and Difficult Urination

Neither of these afflictions should be of concern as they are normal, considering shortage or lack of food, inactivity, and lack of fresh water.

Signals

As in any survival situation all signalling devices should be checked and prepared as soon as possible after boarding the raft. Each item should be tied to the person or the raft so they are not lost in the event of capsizing. They should be kept as dry as possible and ready for immediate use.

Use the emergency radios as directed bearing in mind to conserve the batteries until you are confident search aircraft will be looking for you. In cold climates remember to keep the batteries warm. For multi-place aircraft use the Gibson Girl, as detailed in Chapter 6.

Do not ignite pyrotechnics until an aircraft or ship is seen. When igniting pyros keep them clear of the body and don't allow any of the burning residue to fall on or in the raft.

Use the heliograph mirror any time the sun is shining. Sweep the horizon with it even if a ship or aircraft cannot be seen or heard. An empty ration can (polished up) can be used as an improvised mirror. Cut an X in the center of it and aim the same as the heliograph.

Do not use the sea marker dye until an aircraft or ship is sighted. Activate it as directed on the container. If you are not located the dye marker can be brought aboard and used a second time. Precautions should be taken to prevent it from contaminating your food or water. It can be tied on the outside of the buoyancy chamber of the raft, above the water level.

The signal light should be used at night only. The water activated battery can sometimes be used a second time, if not depleted, by lifting from the water and recapping the holes.

The whistle should be used to attract attention of personnel in the water when originally boarding the raft or in the case of capsizing. It also should be used to attract the attention of passing surface craft, as sound travels well over water.

Water

DO NOT DRINK SEA WATER.

Fresh drinking water will be your most critical requirement. The body requires water to keep functioning for an indefinite period. With no water to drink one can expect to survive only a few days where the humidity of the air is low and the daytime temperature is in the vicinity of 120°F. This survival time without water will increase to approximately 10 days at lower temperatures, at sea, where the humidity is higher. To appreciably increase survival time, water intake must be increased to approximately 4 quarts daily. There are case histories of personnel surviving without drinking water at sea for up to 17 days and others who survived on as little as 2 to 4 oz of water daily. However, these cases are exceptional and one should attempt to consume as much water as thirst dictates to keep the body functioning normally. There is no real advantage to rationing water other than to ensure everyone gets his fair share. Drink but do not waste. Injured personnel should have all they want, if available.

Sources of Drinking Water

   a. your life raft kit contains de-salter kits and in some instances solar stills. Activate these as per instructions on the packets;

   b. rain water—use every means available to catch and store rain water. If salt is dried on the canopy of the raft rinse it in sea water prior to catching rain. The small amount of salt contamination will have no ill effect and in fact will make the rain water more palatable;

   c. dew can be collected on the inside of the raft canopy during the night. This will not produce much water but every bit counts;

   d. icebergs (in the northern hemisphere) are a source of fresh water but should be approached with caution as there is extreme danger in the event they roll over;

   e. old sea ice can be recognized by its clear bluish color and is virtually salt free; and

   f. some survival kits contain canned water.

General Rules

Preserving water in the body is equally as important as consuming water. Following are important rules:

   a. if no water is available—*do not eat.* The process of digestion, particularly proteins, requires water to assimilate;

   b. in hot climates reduce the loss of body water through perspiration, as much as possible. Remain inactive. Dip clothing in sea, wring out and put back on—then use cooling effect of any breeze. If dried salt accumulates on the body it should be brushed off with a dry cloth. Remain in shade as much as possible;

   c. sleep and rest will minimize loss of body fluids;

   d. prevent seasickness if possible. Relax and keep your mind on other chores. Use seasick tablets if available;

   e. do not drink alcohol as it dehydrates the body;

f. smoking increases thirst so if you must smoke do so during the evenings or nights; and

g. to decrease the desire to drink, suck on a button or piece of cloth. This increases the saliva in the mouth.

Food

The amount of food that one may eat in a sea survival situation is in direct proportion to the amount of drinking water available. The body requires water for the digestion process as well as for the elimination of waste products, resulting from eating. Food is not that important that one should be concerned about not eating for several days. The body will continue to function for a long time without food as it will draw on body fats to keep it going. There are two main categories of food in relationship to the balance between food and water.

a. carbohydrates—such as the emergency ration carried in survival kits. This food requires very little water for digestion. If slightly more water is available than is required to maintain a water balance in the system this ration can be eaten as per directions on the ration tin; and

b. proteins—such as fish, shellfish, meat, eggs, and certain greens. This food requires a great deal of water and as a result should not be eaten unless your supply of water is such that you have more than you need to allay normal thirst.

General Rules

a. If you have ample water, eat whatever protein foods that are available first and save your emergency carbohydrate rations for the time that water becomes more scarce;

b. fish will probably be your largest possible source of protein. The juice from fish flesh should not be considered a substitute for drinking water as it contains proteins and will require more water to digest. All sea birds will also be a possible source of protein food. Sea weeds are edible either raw or cooked but remember all of these require extra water for digestion;

c. remember the amount of drinking water you have will determine how much, (if any), food can be eaten; and

d. do not eat if you are inclined to be sea sick as it will merely aggravate the situation.

Subsidizing your Emergency Rations

If you have ample drinking water you should consider subsidizing your emergency rations from the sea.

Most fish in the open sea are edible. Those to avoid are:

a. fish that are brightly colored;
b. fish covered with bristles or spines;
c. fish that puff up;
d. fish with parrot like mouths or humanoid teeth.

Any or all of these can prove to be poisonous. Avoid fish eggs found in clusters or clumps, they will probably be poisonous.

Normal jigging techniques for fishing are recommended or by casting hook out and retrieving hand over hand.

Do not handle fish line with bare hands or tie line to the raft.

All sea birds are edible, either cooked or raw. Birds can be caught on a baited fish hook floating on the surface. They can sometimes be caught as they perch on the raft.

General Dangers of the Sea

In addition to the danger of capsizing or exposure to the elements there are other dangers to guard against.

a. sharks—can be recognized by the fin and tail slicing through the surface of the water. They are attracted by light colored objects, blood, vomit, body waste, and garbage. Keep your feet and hands in the raft and discard garbage etc, in small amounts as far away from the raft as possible, preferably at night. If a shark approaches the raft attempt to scare him off by making loud splashing noises on the surface with anything available. Generally, sharks are only curious unless attracted by the smell of something to eat, they will get into a feeding frenzy and become very dangerous;

b. barracuda—has a similar appearance to a pike. This fish is aggressive, and if seen, the same precautions should be taken as for the shark;

c. swordfish—have a long bill or sword. Although they are not normally dangerous they have been known to ram a boat, if attacked or wounded;

d. killer whale—usually travel in schools. They will be recognized by their sail-like fin cutting the surface of the water as they swim in a porpoising manner. They are black on the back. They will not normally bother a raft, but can overturn a raft if you are in their path; and

e. moray eels, stingrays, poisonous shellfish, and snakes—these will normally be found in the tropics around coral reefs or near shore. Precautions should be taken to ensure hands and feet are covered, when wading ashore.

Precautions in Dealing with Dangerous Fish

a. keep clothing on and keep a good lookout;

b. do not fish if any of the above are in the vicinity;

c. do not trail hands or feet in the water;

d. remain in the raft at all times;

e. do not throw waste food, body waste, etc. overboard during the the day;

f. if dangerous fish are about, remain quiet in the raft and the likelihood of them attacking will be negligible; and

g. if you are in the water, and dangerous fish approach, you should beat the water with strong regular strokes. If a group of survivors are in the water, form a circle facing outwards and beat the water. If there is an injured person keep him inside the circle.

Landfall

It is generally conceded that one should stream the sea anchor with the intent of remaining as close as possible to the scene of the ditching or bail out. This will normally assist search and rescue to find you. However there may be times when you will have to elect to attempt to reach land. A life raft can be sailed up to as much as 10 degrees off wind direction but your course will be governed mainly by ocean currents and wind.

To utilize the ocean current to assist in travelling have all occupants sit as low in the raft as possible, soften the raft somewhat, and stream the sea anchor.

To utilize the wind, if the direction is favourable, top up the raft so it rides higher in the water, have all occupants sit up erect, haul the sea anchor aboard, and empty the ballast pockets. Use anything available for a sail.

Locating Land

Indications of where land may be, can be determined by:

a. cumulus clouds forming in the distance on a clear day, are likely formed over land;
b. birds often fly out to sea in the morning and return to land at night;
c. wind normally blows towards land during the day and reverses in the evening;
d. in the tropics, often the reflection of coral reefs or lagoons will be seen on the underside of clouds or in the sky. This will be in the form of a greenish tint;
e. deep water is dark green or blue. Lighter color indicates shallower water and may be an indication land is near; and
f. drifting wood or vegetation often indicates land is near.

Do not mistake a mirage for land. By changing your height in the raft the mirage will either disappear or change shape.

Landing

If you are sailing or drifting ashore there are precautions to be observed:

a. ensure your life vest is worn and fully inflated;
b. wear all clothing including shoes;
c. pick the best landing point and attempt to manoeuvre towards it;
d. trail the sea anchor with as much line as possible to slow down your approach;
e. try to keep your raft on the seaward side of large waves;
f. stay in the raft until it is grounded on the beach; and
g. once the raft has grounded get out quickly and beach it.

General

Remember that no matter how formidable a sea survival situation may appear you can survive if you possess a strong will to live, keep calm, develop a plan of action, and remember your survival training.

DESERT
SURVIVAL

CHAPTER 13

DESERT SURVIVAL

Introduction

When it is realized that there is at least one desert in each continent of the world, it will be appreciated that the problem of desert survival is a very real one for those who fly over these various areas. One fifth of the land surface of the earth is considered desert and is inhabited by approximately 4 per cent of the world population. There are approximately fifty important deserts. The larger of these are well known: Sahara, Libyan, Arabian, Gobi, and Mongolia.

What is the desert like? It's hot and dry, and it's sparsely inhabited and even more sparsely vegetated. Some of it is mountainous, some of it is sandy, and some areas are gravel. It might be defined as an unfavourable site to terminate a flight.

Desert Hazards

The greatest problem in the desert is lack of water. The amount you require depends on the temperature and your activities, clothing, and shelter. The next problem is exposure to sun and heat, one of the desert's greatest hazards. Day-time temperatures can go as high as 125°F. Exposure to such extreme temperatures can cause heat cramps, heat exhaustion, or heat stroke. The desert sun can complicate this with sunburn or sunblindness or both. The scarceness of animal and vegetable life in the desert makes it nearly impossible to rely on replenishing your food supplies from these sources. Another irritating problem is insects. Flies and sand flies can be bothersome, and mosquitoes may carry malaria.

Immediate Actions after Emergency Landing

Water will be your biggest problem if you are down in the desert. Therefore, on leaving the aircraft when it comes to rest, take all your water if possible and your safety equipment packs. Stay well away from the crashed aircraft until all fire hazards have passed.

Get into the shade as soon as possible, and keep your head and the back of your neck covered. Evaluate the situation calmly and decide on your course of action. Don't rush, take it easy. The two things that require your immediate attention are first aid and shelter.

First Aid

Attend promptly to all injuries. Move all injured personnel into the shade as soon as possible. Follow the established first aid practices.

Exposure to the desert sun is dangerous. It can cause heat cramps, heat exhaustion, heat stroke, and a serious sunburn.

Protect the eyes to prevent sunblindness. Symptoms are burning, watering, or inflamed eyes, headaches, and poor vision. Treat sunblindness by protecting the eyes from light and relieving the pain. Place the patient in a dark shelter or cover the eyes with a light-proof bandage.

Water

Water is the key to survival in the desert. If you are lucky you may have a good supply in your aircraft. If not your chances of finding a good supply may be slim.

If you are near an oasis, your water problem may be solved early. They are low spots characterized by vegetation.

If you are near the coast, fresh water can sometimes be found in the dunes above the beach or even under the surface of the beach itself. Look in the hollows between dunes for water which may have collected there. If you don't find it there, dig down on the leeward side of the first dune or any place where the sand appears moist. The first water you encounter will probably be fresh. If you get salt water you must not drink it.

If inland, look for dry river beds. They may produce water by digging below the concave bank on the outside of a curve or bend. Allow the water to collect by scooping small holes.

Another source of water is dew which can be collected early in the morning from rocks and metals. You may sop up the dew with a piece of cloth and then wring it out. Another method of obtaining water is illustrated below.

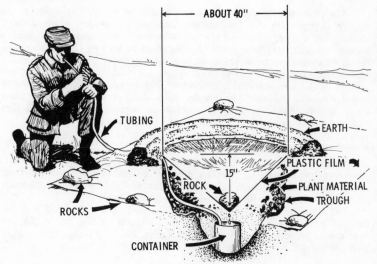

A water still made out of a tin can and a sheet of clear plastic can produce up to 3 pints of water a day out of hot desert sands. The still is made by digging a hole, placing a can or other container in the bottom, and covering the hole with a sheet of plastic.

The centre of the plastic is pushed down to form a cone over the can. As air under the plastic gets hot, moisture from the ground evaporates to condense on the underside of the plastic, and the drops running down the plastic will collect in the container.

A tube can be inserted in the can and run to the surface to enable drinking from the container without disturbing the still.

Obtaining water is only half the battle. You must make it last by conserving perspiration. The body gets rid of heat through evaporation or perspiration. As the body fluids drop, perspiration is reduced, body temperatures go up, and efficiency is drastically reduced. An increase of six degrees from normal temperature is fatal. Although it may feel cooler with your clothes off, you are losing body fluids rapidly. Being fully clothed keeps the heat out, and slows evaporation. The main points to remember are drink water and preserve perspiration to avoid dehydrating. The water chart at the end of this chapter will provide an idea of your daily water requirement.

Signals

Your aircraft radio or emergency set will be your best rescue aid. Ground signals should be laid out to make your position as conspicuous as possible. Full use should be made of coloured equipment which will form a contrast with the natural surroundings. Signal equipment should be kept ready for immediate use as soon as an aircraft is heard.

Shelter

One of your first requirements will be shelter from the sun and heat. Natural shelter is limited to the shade of cliffs or the leeside of hills. In some desert mountains, you may find cavelike protection under tumbled rocks broken from cliff sides. Caves and the walls of stream beds provide a source of shade.

If you remain with the aircraft, don't use the inside of it for shelter in the daytime. The fuselage will be too hot. Use the wing of the aircraft, with a parachute or any other cloth as an awning. Be sure to leave approximately two feet of open space below the canopy for air circulation. Make sure the aircraft is securely moored and that there is no chance of its collapsing during high winds or a storm.

A covered trench will also provide shade, but again there must be space for air circulation.

In some desert areas the aircraft fuselage may be used as a shelter during the desert winter. It gets cold during the night while the daytime temperatures are about 90°F.

Fires

Fires are rarely required in the desert except to purify water, to boil tea, and for signalling.

Fuel is usually extremely rare and aircraft oil and fuel will be most useful if available. Fire building is not difficult. Stoves can be made out of any metal container or by building stones in a small circle. Fill the container with sand, saturate it with oil or gasoline, and then carefully light with a match. Holes should be made in the container to provide ventilation. Never add petroleum fuels to a fire already started or even smouldering.

All twigs, leaves, stems, and underground roots may be used for fuel if you are able to locate plant growth. Dried animal dung may also be used as fuel.

Clothing

Don't discard any of your clothing. You require it for protection against sunburn, heat, sand, and insects. Keep your head, neck, and body covered during the day, and you'll last longer on less water. Wear loose, light-coloured clothing if possible, using parts of parachutes if available. Your T-shirt makes a good neck drape. If you have no hat make one from a parachute or any other material available, similar to the type worn by the Arabs. You can adapt a pilot chute for use as a parasol.

Eyes must be protected from both direct and reflected glare. Sunglasses must be worn throughout the day. If they are not available a piece of cloth with slits cut for the eyes (just large enough to allow a penny to pass through) makes a good eyeshield. Smearing soot under the eyes helps to reduce the glare.

Your feet should be kept in good shape. Rest your feet often. Remove shoes, dry out socks and turn them inside out, and try to keep the inside of shoes free from sand. If your shoes wear out, or you lose them, improvise a type of sandal from aircraft rubber flooring, parachute material, or any other available material.

If you are caught in a dust storm, cover your mouth and nose. Button up your clothing tightly, and lie down back to the wind. To avoid sand from drifting around you, roll about from time to time.

Owing to the extremes in temperatures, the need for additional clothing will be felt at night.

Food

Food on the desert is always a problem. First check the aircraft for any ration packs or fresh food. Any open foods or opened rations should be eaten first as they will not keep long.

Although birds and animals are scarce in areas with little water or vegetation, they may sometimes be found. Small burrowing animals come out at dawn or dusk and can be caught in snares.

Edible plant food is rare in the desert. Grasses are edible, and some areas have edible wild tulips or onions. Avoid plants with milky or coloured saps as they are likely to be poisonous. Remember the rules with regard to eating if water is scarce.

Travel

The decision to travel or remain with the aircraft will in all likelihood be difficult to make. Travel should be undertaken only if it is certain that the objective can be reached on the water supply available. Do not underestimate the difficulties that will be encountered or overestimate your physical condition.

After it is decided to travel, ensure that you don't overload. Carry only the essential items. Your total load should not exceed 35 lbs. Water and a shelter will be your main items. Suggested items are: a light material to provide shelter; a parachute canopy if available; compass, signal mirror, and signal devices; map; pencil; knife; salt; sun-glasses; first aid kit; a watch; and a flashlight.

During the desert summer you'll travel only at night and rest during the day. Don't hurry, follow the easiest route, and avoid soft sand areas and rough terrain as much as possible. Determine your position accurately and mark it on the map before setting out. Decide on a course and stick to it. Your compass and the stars will be your greatest navigational aids. When deciding your objective, it is best to choose one that is easy to find, such as a coast or road which can be followed until habitation is reached, rather than a specific point like an oasis which may be very difficult to find or pinpoint.

Natives

Another important phase of desert survival is obtaining assistance from others. If you can contact any of the natives who live on the desert, your chances of survival will greatly increase. Generally their sense of hospitality is very strong, and they will provide you with water, food, and shelter. Their customs and religion are much different from ours, so try not to offend them in any way.

Desert survival is difficult but by no means impossible. However, you must be ready to solve the problems of water and exposure as well as the other desert hazards.

DAILY WATER REQUIREMENT TO MAINTAIN WATER BALANCE

Mean Temperature Degrees F	Pints per 24 Hours
95	9
90	$6\frac{1}{2}$
85	$4\frac{1}{2}$
80	$2\frac{1}{2}$
75	2

In the desert the mean temperature can be taken as 15°F below the daily maximum.

In hot deserts you need a minimum of a gallon of water a day. If you walk in the cool desert night you can get approximately 20 miles for that daily gallon. If you travel in day-time heat, you'll be lucky to get 10 miles to the gallon.

TROPICAL
SURVIVAL

CHAPTER 14

TROPICAL SURVIVAL

Introduction

Uninhabited tropical areas are not as difficult to survive in as many people believe. Some people visualize the tropics as an enormous and forbidding jungle through which each step taken must be hacked out. Actually, much of the tropics is not jungle. It is true that travel in jungle areas is very difficult, but normally there is little danger from animals. Tropical terrain varies from forest jungle, mangrove, or other swamps to open grassy plains or semi-arid bushland.

The real dangers of the tropics are not the animals or snakes, which most people have heard wild tales about, but rather the insects. Many of the insects carry infection and disease. One of the worst diseases is malaria transmitted by the mosquito. Many people are frightened by the howls, screams, and other sounds made by birds, animals, and insects. However, this is only psychological and usually no real danger exists.

Immediate Action

The first decision to be made after a crash landing will probably be whether to travel or stay with the aircraft. If a landing is made in an area where neither the aircraft nor signals can be easily sighted from the air and if there are no injuries, then probably it would be wise to travel.

Injuries must be taken care of first. In tropical areas even the slightest scratch can cause a serious infection within hours, so first aid is the first requirement after landing. Don't leave the crash area without carefully blazing or marking a route so that you can return to the crash site or others can follow your trail.

Shelter

Night in the jungle comes very quickly, so prepare for bed early. In the jungle more rest and sleep are required to keep up energy and strength in order to maintain resistance to disease.

Try to locate a camp site on a knoll or high spot in a clearing well away from the swamps. There will be fewer mosquitoes and other insects, and the ground will be dryer. Such an area will be necessary for ground signals too.

Do not plan to sleep on the ground. Construct a bed by covering a pile of brush with layers of palm fronds or other broad leaves. A better bed can be constructed by making a frame of poles and covering the top with long, spineless, palm leaves, to a depth of four or five layers. Cut the corner upright poles long enough to support a mosquito net or parachute covering. A hammock provides a good type of bed and can be made from a parachute strung between two trees.

A good rainproof shelter can be built by covering an A-type framework with a good thickness of palm or other broad leaf, pieces of bark, or mats of grass. This is similar to a brush type lean-to made from spruce boughs, only it has two sides instead of one.

If you stay with your aircraft, it may be used for a shelter and will probably provide a dry area in the wet jungle forest. Try to make it mosquito proof by covering the opening with netting or parachute material.

Do not camp too near a stream or pond, especially during the rainy season. Do not build a shelter under dead trees or with dead limbs, nor under a coconut tree. A falling coconut can disable a person.

Clothing protects against exposure, insects, and pests. Keep the pant cuffs tucked into the tops of the stockings, and tie them securely or improvise puttees to keep out ticks and leeches. Keep sleeves rolled down and buttoned. This also helps to protect against scratches from thorns, brambles, etc.

When clothes are removed, make a thorough inspection of the body for ticks, chiggers, insects, leeches, or any other vermin. Check the clothing too, and remove any insects that may have got on it.

Try to have the clothing dry before nightfall to avoid discomfort from the cold. It is most important to keep clothing clean, dry, and in good repair. Dirty clothes not only rot quickly but may lead to skin disease.

Signals

As in most other survival situations the aircraft radio, if working, is the best signal device. Emergency radios are not very efficient in jungle areas. Pyros should be kept handy and dry. A signal area may be very difficult to find. However, parachutes or contrasting coloured objects such as dinghies stretched across streams or bays or placed in ponds may attract attention. Smoke or fire signals in clearings are also effective. Make use of every signal device that is available.

Fires

A fire in the jungle is most desirable. It provides warmth during chilly nights, serves for cooking, and helps keep away mosquitoes and curious animals. A big roaring fire is not necessary, because a small one serves the same purpose and is easier to maintain.

Fuel is usually plentiful. The fire lighting problem may be difficult during the rainy season when dry fuel is hard to locate. Many of the large trees whether dead or alive have hollow trunks. Cut strips of the dry inner lining for tinder. When the fire is going well, wet wood can be added. Dry wood may be found hanging in the network of vines or lying on bushes.

Don't use bamboo for fuel. It burns too quickly, emits dangerous fumes, and may explode.

Good tinder may be found in the fibres at the bases of palm leaves. The inside of termite nests also makes good kindling. Keep a good supply of wood handy, and keep it dry by stowing it in your shelter or beneath broad green leaves. Dry out wet kindling and fuel near your fire.

Food and Water

Normally both food and water are plentiful in the tropics. Water is available from the numerous streams, springs, lakes, pools, and swamps, but it is not safe to drink until it has been purified. Some water may be discoloured or turbid and may be partially cleared by filtering through an improvised filter such as parachute cloth. One may also obtain water from some plants which can be used without further treatment. Coconuts contain water, and the green unripe coconuts about the size of a grapefruit are the best. In addition vines are often a good source of water; however never drink from a vine that has a milky sap. Water may also be collected during a rain by digging a hole and lining it with a tarpaulin or a piece of canvas.

Animal trails often lead to water. Food is usually easy to procure in the jungle. There are usually a number of different types of fruits and vegetables. Some of the common edible ones are: sago palm or palm cabbage; bananas; bamboo shoots; coconuts; and papaya. Any food a monkey eats can be eaten by man.

There are edible fish in most of the jungle streams. You need have no fear about poisonous fish because they are found only in salt water.

Travel

Travel in the tropics can be difficult because of heavy undergrowth, heat and humidity, swamps, mangroves, and the lack of landmarks.

The most useful aids to travel are: a machete to help cut a route; find food, and make a raft; a compass; a first aid kit in case of fever or infection; good foot-gear; and a hammock or material to construct one.

If possible follow the downward flow of a stream as it likely flows towards larger bodies of water and consequently towards settlements. When possible, construct a raft from bamboo or light wood and float down the stream, as this is the fastest and easiest method of transportation in tropical forest areas.

Avoid such obstacles as thickets, mangroves, and swamps. Stop early and prepare a night camp as it gets dark early and quickly in the tropics.

KNOTS AND SPLICES

CHAPTER 15

KNOTS AND SPLICES

Knot Requirements

The four basic requirements for knots are:

(a) they must be easy to tie or untie;

(b) they can be tied in the middle of a length of rope;

(c) they can be tied when the rope is under tension; and

(d) they can be tied in such a fashion that the rope will not cut itself when under strain.

Classes of Knots

There are five basic classes of knots. They are used for:

(a) joining two ends of rope of the same diameter (reef);

(b) joining two ends of rope of different diameters (bends);

(c) forming running loops (bowline group);

(d) forming stationary loops (bowline group); and

(e) securing one end of the rope to a point (hitches).

a Thumb Knot.
Stops unlaying of the
rope.

b Figure of Eight.
Prevents the rope
from being pulled
through the pulley.

c Reef Knot.
For joining two
ropes of equal
diameter.

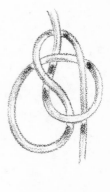

d Sheet Bend.
   For joining two
   ropes of unequal
   diameters.

e Hawser Bend.
   For tying two
   large ropes
   together.

f Bowline.
   For making a non-
   slip loop in the
   end of a rope.

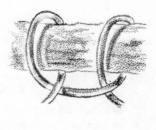

g Running Bowline.
   For making a running loop
   in the end of a rope.

h Clove Hitch.
   Mooring knot.

j Timber Hitch.
  For hauling or towing
  timber.

k Round Turn—Two Half
  Hitches.
  Mooring knot.

l Sheep Shank.
  For shortening a rope that
  is tied at both ends.

Splices

Back Splice

(a) unlay the rope for approximately eight inches at the end;

(b) make the crown knot;

(c) splice the ends of the rope into the main rope, taking them over one and under the next one;

(d) when all three strands have been spliced in once, this is known as a tuck;

(e) carry out this procedure for four full tucks;

(f) then split the strands in half and taking one half of each strand do two more tucks—these are called half tucks, because you use only half the rope, which tapers off the end of the splice;

(g) do this by starting a half inch above the cut ends and pulling the cord as tight as possible and keeping the turns close together while working away from the end of the rope to a half inch past the end of the splice.

Crown Knot

Back Splice

204

Short Splice

    (a) unlay both ends of the rope for eight inches;

    (b) marry the ends of the rope where the unlaying stops by putting the strands of one end of the rope between the strands of the other end of the rope;

    (c) splice by going over one and under one with all six strands;

    (d) carry out this procedure three more times;

    (e) divide each strand in half and do two half tucks with the half strands;

    (f) cut off all strands to within a half inch; and

    (g) serve the splice with cord, starting three quarters of an inch above the start of the splice and ending a half inch below the splice.

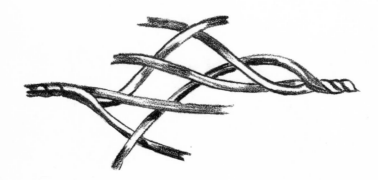